"You have in your hands more than a mere book. This is a tool, a collection of road tested wisdom, insight, and heart to help America get unstuck. White privilege, as a system, is too often obscured and swept under every societal rug that can be constructed. Here, it is not only out and discussed; here is community, hope and practice to change it."

- Makani Themba,

Author, Organizer and Revolutionary Grandmother at The Praxis Project and the Minister of Revolutionary Imagination of the 'Other America's' Department of Arts and Culture

"While Chris Crass' work may be perceived by many in the Black Lives Matter Movement as that of working primarily with White allies, each of us can learn something from his tenacity and passion for [t]his kind of justice work. For those of us who call ourselves Christian, Chris Crass is one of the 'voices crying out in the wilderness' urging us to 'act justly and to love mercy and to walk humbly with our God' [Micah 6:8]. Chris often presses us to move beyond the stereotypical understandings of race, class, and gender to a place of discomfort, which can become the catalyst for change. Kudos for forcing us to look into the dreaded mirror to take a glimpse of what 'awakened souls' can do when we work together."

- The Rev. Maxine Allen,
Ordained Elder United Methodist Church

"White people need to read this so that they have an opportunity to grasp the seriousness of this situation. It has to involve us all, with leadership by the people most affected and actively supported by the rest of the people, with the understanding that comes out of reading this book. This is a book written by a good, honest, sincere, trustworthy white man, who has taken up the battle from a strong, supportive, and involved position. He is fighting with the community and you can feel his strength as you talk with him and look in his eyes, and you'll feel it reading this book."

- Miss Major griffin-gracy,

Black, Trans-Woman, Elder, Movement Leader from Stonewall to Today with "BlackTransLivesMatter". She is the subject of the new documentary, MAJOR

"Chris Crass brings a level of honesty, vulnerability, transparency and all together audacious authenticity to his work against oppression and white supremacy. This is not something I have found with many white men writers. I would suggest that everyone read his book. Especially persons serious about working across race towards building Beloved Community."

- Tufara Waller Muhammad,
Cultural Organizer with the Arkansas Women's Project and Datule' Artist Collective

Towards the "Other America"

ANTI-RACIST RESOURCES FOR WHITE PEOPLE
TAKING ACTION FOR BLACK LIVES MATTER

Chris Crass

CHALICE
PRESS

ST. LOUIS, MISSOURI

Towards the "Other America": Anti-Racist Resources for White People Taking Action for Black Lives Matter

Cover design: Aisha Shillingford

Cover photos: Nate Royko Maurer. Young, Gifted and Black marches in Madison, WI.

Christopher L. Walton/UUA. Die-in civil disobedience June 27th, 2015, during the Unitarian Universalist (UU) General Assembly in Portland Oregon. From left to right: UU minister Elizabeth Nguyen, Rev. Osagyefo Sekou of Fellowship of Reconciliation, UU young adult leader Amanda Weatherspoon, and Chris Crass.

National Archives & Records Administration, Photograph of Civil Rights March on Washington,1963.

www.ChalicePress.com

Paperback: 9780827237094

EPDF: 9780827237117

For Ella Baker and Anne Braden, and the organizing tradition they passed on to us.

For my sons River and August and the Beloved Community we are building for all of our children.

Ella Baker and Anne Braden leaving Civil Rights movement strategy meeting at the Highlander Center

Abernathy Children on the front line leading the march from Selma to Montgomery for the Right to Vote, 1965

Table of Contents

The "Other America"

"**I** call what I joined 'the other America.' This other America has always existed, even before the slave ships arrived. African Americans have always fought against their oppression, and many died rather than endure slavery. And at least some whites have joined these struggles – in the early resistance to slavery, the Abolitionist movement, the Reconstruction period after the Civil War, the upsurges of people's movements in the 1930s, the civil rights activities of the 1950s and '60s, and beyond to today in the 21st century.

And this resistance actually has roots that stretch back to the beginning of the human race. In every age, no matter how cruel the oppression carried on by those in power, there have been those who struggled for a different world. I believe this is the genius of humankind, the thing that makes us half divine: the fact that some human beings can envision a world that has never existed. Perhaps no one living today will see a major change. But it will come. And living in that world that is working to make it happen lets us know that our lives are worthwhile."

Anne Braden, longtime white Southern anti-racist organizer

For White Anti-Racist Leadership and a World Where Black Lives Matter: The Purpose of This Book

We are living in monumental times. This is a book for white people who want to rise up against racism and work for a world where Black lives matter. This is a book for white people who have recently come into consciousness about the devastating reality of racism and want to take action. It is also a book for white people who have a long history of working for justice and want to step up and be more effective in this time of large scale, grassroots, Black liberation movement. In short, this book is for white people who want to take courageous action for racial justice; it is for those who want to be part of truly life-affirming liberation movements, and build up the world based on our deepest values of the inherent worth and dignity of all people, the interconnection of all of life, and the sacredness of this world.

But first, why is this a book written by a white person, for white people, when this is about the Black Lives Matter movement? I was radicalized by the Rodney

BLM direct action in Toronto, Canada. Photo: Jalani Morgan

King verdict in Los Angeles, in which four white police officers were acquitted for brutally beating a Black man, Rodney King. The largest uprising in the U.S., in a generation, erupted in Los Angeles following the verdict and my colorblind, post-racial framework was up in flames just like the city thirty minutes from my house. As I got more and more involved in multiracial racial justice work, protested against police brutality, marched for immigrant rights, and engaged in Ethnic Studies, the more I heard leaders of color talk about the importance of white people working in white communities to end racism. The call was to build up a base of support for racial justice in white communities, so that we could then form powerful multiracial coalitions.

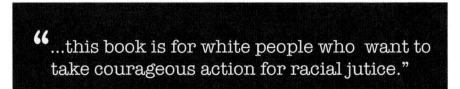

"...this book is for white people who want to take courageous action for racial jutice."

I studied the Civil Rights movement and learned about the Student Nonviolent Coordinating Committee of the 1960s. I learned that they called on white people to both support the Black-led Civil Rights movement and to return to white communities to free white people's minds from white supremacy. They developed anti-racist white efforts that could then unite, as equals, with Black organizations, rather than the traditional model of white people thinking their job was to tell Black Civil Rights workers what to do. Around this time, I found mentors like David Rojas, Sharon Martinas, Roxanne Dunbar-Ortiz, Elizabeth 'Betita' Martinez, Paul Kivel, and Linda Burnham, who helped me understand the strategy of working against racism in the white community. I developed white anti-racist leadership with the goal of building powerful grassroots movements that could advance an overall agenda of economic, racial, gender, and social justice for all. I studied white anti-racist Civil Rights movement organizers like Anne and Carl Braden in Kentucky and Zilphia and Myles Horton in Tennessee, all of whom emphasized the importance of moving white people into action for racial justice.

In 2000, I joined with a crew of younger generation white activists in the global justice movement to form the Catalyst Project in the San Francisco Bay Area. With the support of older mentors from the Civil Rights, Black Power, Chicano Power, and Women's Liberation movements, we worked with thousands of white activists around the country to develop anti-racist leadership. We did this just as organizers of color had called for historically, as they encouraged us to do in our lives, to work against racism in the white community so that we could then bring large numbers of white people into multiracial movements. We invited them into what we increasingly began calling collective liberation. Collective liberation is a concept I first heard from bell hooks who talks about the interconnection of systems of oppression in the form of white supremacist capitalist patriarchy. For me, as a white person challenging racism and as a man working for feminism, I began to see myself in a vision of interconnected systems of liberation.

The more I worked in white communities against racism and for racial justice with a collective liberation vision, the more it became spiritual work. It was spiritual as I began to see and experience the devastation of white supremacy on white communities. I had seen it in my own family, in my Grandfather and in my uncles: the resentment and anger towards Black and Brown communities, anger and resentment that was toxic and ate away at their and other white people's humanity, their sense of justice, safety, and democracy in the world. Now, as a father with two young white boys, I understand anti-racist work as fighting against the monstrosity of white supremacy that steals the lives of Black and Brown children and devours the humanity of white children.

Not My Ozarks anti-racist, anti-Klan campaign. Photo: Rachel Luster

This book is a compilation of short essays and notes written to white activists on questions of anti-racist organizing since the uprising in Ferguson after the murder of Michael

" It is often in the unfamiliar histories and concepts that we can find hope and purpose."

Brown. It is also a compilation of interviews I conducted with white racial justice organizers around the country to help make anti-racist work tangible, concrete, and replicable. The focus of the interviews is on lessons for organizing white people in Black Lives Matter movement times. In addition to the writing, I also wanted to weave in images of white people taking action for racial justice and Black Lives Matter. These images are from around the country—images of everyday extraordinary people to inspire us all.

This book was made to help equip white people to join in the Black Lives Matter movement and to bring anti-racist leadership into white communities, institutions, organizations, congregations, and families. My goal is to help support white people to join with others to work against structural inequality, build up beloved community, and work for the abolition of anti-Black racism. This book is here to help white people be courageous for racial justice, which is key to getting us all free. Some of you reading this book will be familiar with the concepts used, and the social justice organizations referenced. Some of you won't be. I know that unfamiliar terms and references can be off-putting, like a gate meant to keep you out. I encourage you, if you stumble upon the unfamiliar, keep going. It is often in the unfamiliar histories and concepts that we can find hope and purpose.

There is a reason why many of us know obscure trivia about the rich and famous, yet know very little about people's movements for liberation. There is a reason why many of us are far more familiar with insecurity, self-doubt, and even self-hatred, than we are with the feelings of community, solidarity, self-love, and liberation. Those who have the power to rule, those who have the power to accumulate vast amounts of wealth from vast numbers of people's labor, do not want people knowing the history or the politics of liberation movements. Those who rule want those who are ruled to internalize the logic of supremacy so that the ruled not only stay in their place in the hierarchy of power, but blame the people below them for the misery generated by inequality rather than those at the top who profit from it. My hope with this book is that unfamiliar terms and references serve as keys to open doors, to help us come together and work more effectively for racial justice.

We live in historic times. From the uprisings in Ferguson and Baltimore, to the campaigns that demand justice for Sandra Bland and Tamir Rice. Millions of people are taking action against racism. With working class and poor people rising up in the Black community and visionary Black women like Alicia Garza, Patrisse Cullors, and Opal Tometi bringing not only new leadership, but new styles of leadership, we are living in a time of the Black liberation movement on the move. With campaigns like #SayHerName and #BlackTransLivesMatter, this is a feminist movement, a queer movement, and an intersectional movement.

Black women's lives matter.
Black trans people's lives matter.
Black disabled people's lives matter.
Black poor people's lives matter.

"You are needed to help bring this leadership."

This is a movement to remake the world with the values of everyday people's liberation made central rather than the heartless logic of supremacist systems, the logic of white supremacist capitalist patriarchy.

While these times are full of heartbreak and pain, they are also full of possibility and hope. For, it is not the racist murder of Black people that is new, it is that there is a Black Lives Matter movement uniting millions of people in saying "No More! Another world where Black lives matter is possible." And white people all over the country are questioning the white supremacist lies, are opening their minds and hearts to new understandings of the world, and are horrified by racist violence. White anti-racist leadership is needed to help move those white people towards racial justice and away from the agenda of death and structural inequality.

Far too often the most vocal and passionate voices in white communities talking about race are racists. We have seen white anti-racists around the country protest "white silence – consent," but, still, many white anti-racists are afraid or don't know how to end that silence by speaking courageously and passionate about racial justice and refusing to let white supremacy continue to devour the lives of children of color and deform the humanity of white children.

You are needed to help bring this leadership—in your community, place of worship, workplace, school, toddler story time at the library, unions, and the organizations and networks you are part of. It is my prayer that this book, the stories, and interviews within it help you become as powerful as you can be, to end white silence and speak up for and work for a world where Black lives matter, a world rooted in collective liberation—a world where we all get free, together.

Wisconsin Pride. Photo: Bevo Buhr

Shutting Down Oakland, CA Police Department.
Photo: Felicia Gustin

We Must Awaken the Souls of White People to Resist White Supremacy

For those of us who are white in the wake of the Charleston Massacre, an atrocity that sparked national outcry in the long history of the racist violence of the United States, it is not the time for us to call for racial tolerance, racial healing, racial dialogue, or racial understanding alone. When white people say these things, even with the best of intentions, the underlying message undermines Black rage. It erases Black pain and Black resistance and serves white people's guilt and grief with vague gestures that do more to confuse rather than clarify both the problem and the solution.

Rabbis and Jewish activists march in Ferguson, MO. Photo: Margaret Ernst

We need white people leveraging whatever positions of influence they have to put forward—declarations, poems, letters, blog posts, and personal invitations for other white people to join in anti-racist resistance and struggle against the evil of institutional racism. We don't need messages from white people yearning for reconciliation unless it is joined with a courageous call for white people to hear Black rage, follow Black-led resistance, and get active for racial justice.

For those of us who are white and have been engaged in anti-racist efforts, we need to support other white people to tap into their grief, pain, and sadness about Charleston and turn it into a commitment to the destruction and abolition of institutional racism. No calls for healing disconnected from militant resistance from white people against this brutal racist society. No messages meant to soothe white people's souls, and ease them/us back to sleep. We need messages and leadership to help build the capacity of white people to stay in discomfort, to stay in the dis-ease to truly hear and listen to the voices and experiences of Black people, with the goal of putting raised consciousness into action against racism.

Banner hang in Los Angeles, CA. Photo: Jason David

Beloved community isn't born of white hand-wringing but white hands going to work for revolutionary racial justice change. We need white anti-racist agitation, leadership, vision, and strategy, and anger grounded in love for the Black Lives Matter movement and collective liberation. We can do this. I believe in us.

"Beloved community isn't born of white hand-wringing but white hands going to work for revolutionary racial justice change."

Rally Against the Aryan Brotherhood, St. Louis, MO. Photo: Janey Archey

The Heart of Black Lives Matter and Why "All Lives Matter" Is Part of the Problem

The Black Lives Matter movement isn't a contest over whose lives matter more. Throughout history, the right wing has made every attempt to portray Black-led struggles for freedom and equality as Black people trying to get "special rights" by taking something away from white people. From anti-slavery, anti-lynching, anti-discrimination, Civil Rights, and racial justice struggles, the right has mobilized the economic anxiety, fear, and anger of white people and blamed people of color for declining wages, rising costs, and the unraveling of public institutions (which is blamed on people of color and is actually because of massive defunding).

This is how anti-Black racism and white supremacy operate. They are not biologically based, natural reactions of inherently distrustful people and cultures. Anti-Black racism and white supremacy are divide-and-rule strategies developed out of the fear of the U.S. slave society's ruling class—who witnessed indentured Europeans and enslaved Africans unite and fight back, witnessed people of European and African descent marrying and building family together.

Anti-Black racism and white supremacy were developed through laws, policies, and brutal institutionalized violence to keep the vast majority of us fighting and hating each other, while the 1% and those with the power to rule consolidated wealth and power, extracting it from working class communities, with communities of color hardest hit.

The heart of Black Lives Matter is not a fight over whose lives matter more. It is a fight to end institutionalized premature death in the Black community. Premature death because of institutional racism in housing, healthcare, jobs, education, the criminal justice system, and so on. And premature death in acts of relentless and heartbreaking racist violence.

This racist violence does not require the shooter to hate Black people; rather, it only requires they react from the deeply internalized fear of Black bodies, and sense of ownership over Black bodies, on which this society is based: a society built on the slave system which demonized, exploited, and brutalized Black bodies, from the elderly to the babies.

Of course "all lives matter." That is why we are fighting to end the structural premature death of Black people in a racist society. To assert that All Lives Matter in reaction and opposition to Black Lives Matter is just the logic of the slave society, dividing people who should be coming together for a world where all our babies can grow up loved, healthy, resourced, and protected.

All Lives Matter is the new "special rights" smear tactic utilized by the White Citizen's Councils and Klan against the Civil Rights movement. Which side are you on? To those who argue "all lives matter," remember, just as we look back on those who declared "Segregation Today, Segregation Tomorrow, Segregation Forever," history will see you.

Rally Against Police Brutality at the Texas State Capital. Photo: Hannah Williams

Building Power for Racial Justice in White Communities: From Awareness of White Privilege to Anti-Racist Organizing

an interview with Chris Crass by Katy Otto for Feministing

....

Working class communities rally in Dardanelle, AR. Photo: Meredith Martin-Moates

Katy Otto: Tell us a little about yourself.

Chris Crass: I'm a dad, partner, son, author, activist, and social justice movement builder. I'm a white guy, economically in the precarious middle class. My politics come out of the working class anarchist movement of the late 1800s, the Black radical tradition from Harriet Tubman to Ida B. Wells to Angela Davis, the Southern anti-racist socialist tradition, the people's movements of the 1960s

> **" I believe this work is sacred."**

and '70s, women of color feminism, and my Unitarian Universalist faith tradition. I believe in the inherent worth and dignity of all people, the interconnection of life, and that beloved community is nourished through the vast array of labor and love for justice. I'm committed to a vision and strategy of collective liberation, and I believe this work is sacred. I grew up in between the multiracial progressive city of Los Angeles and the suburbs of the right-wing bastion of Orange County, in Southern California. This was during the presidency of Ronald Reagan and the right-wing backlash to the gains of people's movements—in the U.S. Backlash to the gains for civil rights, feminism, economic justice, queer liberation, racial justice, and people's anti-colonial movements for self-determination around the world.

I grew up with parents who raised me with feminist, social justice values. These values flourished in high school when I became best friends with Mike Rejniak, a working class anarchist punk rock activist. We recruited and joined with others to build up a vibrant counter-cultural youth movement rooted in anarchist/socialist/feminist values and commitments.

Those experiences helped shape the activism, writing, movement building, and, more recently, parenting I've engaged in over the past 25 years. I have three primary focuses in my life.

First, to build powerful working class-based, feminist, multiracial movements for collective liberation.

Second, to organize and write with a focus on moving large numbers of white people towards a multiracial democratic racial/economic justice agenda, large numbers of men towards a feminist/gender justice agenda, and people of various class backgrounds towards a socialist agenda rooted in working class organizing and movements.

Third, to help build and nurture my family with liberation values/culture as part of a larger beloved community that loves kids and honors the magic of childhood.

SURJ Families Protest in Louisville, KY. Photo: Carla Wallace

Katy: Where and when did you first hear the term "white privilege"? What were some of your initial thoughts about it?

Chris: I first read about it in the journal Race Traitor in the early '90s. Race Traitor was an awesome journal about the historical and social construction of whiteness as a ruling class strategy to unite people racialized as white to unite across class behind a ruling class worldview and agenda of structural inequality and violence. The term racialize or racialization highlights the fact that race isn't biologically based; rather, it is socially and politically developed in relationship to the economy. Therefore, Race Traitor argued that if white supremacy and whiteness were created, they could also be destroyed. What has been done, can be undone. I was reading this journal because our high school activist group was part of the Love and Rage Revolutionary

" I knew that my life could never be the same."

Anarchist Federation. Love and Rage was involved nationally in anti-racist work and published a lot of great writing about white supremacy and racial justice struggles.

Some of these essays were written by folks in Race Traitor, and this helped us locally, as a mostly white group of activists, to think about our work against police brutality and immigrant rights.

The real turning point that powerfully impacted my life, political work, and understanding of white privilege, though, was the Rodney King verdict in the spring of 1992 and the rebellion—civil unrest—in Los Angeles that followed. On the night of the verdict, with Los Angeles in flames and tens of thousands of people protesting in the streets, my friend Terence Priester, the one Black person in our group, opened his heart and shared stories of racism he'd experienced, with a gathering of us at my parents' house. Hearing his stories of what we would now call racial profiling was devastating and eye opening. He demolished the colorblind framework I had grown up with, and I knew that my life could never be the same.

It was out of these experiences that I started learning about white privilege, and it made sense, and began to see it all around me. I started thinking about white privilege in my own life and, years later, through continued activist experience and study, began to see how it was negatively impacting my social justice efforts. I began seeing how white privilege was keeping me away from multiracial racial justice efforts. This was because a white privileged worldview prevented me from being able to see, experience, connect with, learn from, and build with leadership and organizing in communities of color. Furthermore, white privilege reinforced a narrative of white people having all the right answers, and best ways of protesting and being an activist.

Katy: How and when do you use the phrase in your own life and activism?

Chris: I think the concept of white privilege as part of a larger understanding of historical and structural white supremacy is crucial, but I think there are lots of ways to talk about it without using the phrase itself. Here's how I think about that.

Our key objective is to bring people together across divisions of race, class, gender, sexuality, ability, citizenship, and age so that we can see and affirm one another's humanity. From that place of connection, we can more powerfully work for an agenda of collective liberation—an agenda that seeks economic, racial, gender, disability, environmental, and social justice for all. This is a vision we won't fully realize, but a vision to help us fight against the nightmare of current injustice and help bring these dreams more and more into existence.

We want to bring people together to work for this vision, and members of the ruling classes know that such unity could lead to their downfall, so those in ruling class power have done all they can to undermine and destroy such unity. One of the first people to start talking about what we now call white privilege was W.E.B. Du Bois. Du Bois is one of the great American intellectuals of the 1900s who studied racism and what he called the "color line" that divides people. He wrote in his book Black Reconstruction that one of the ways racism operates is that it rewards white working class and white poor people with the "psychological wages of whiteness" in exchange for siding with the ruling class. In doing this, white working class and white poor people routinely fight against and suppress the power, dignity, and humanity of other working class and poor people who are of color.

Essentially, Du Bois argues that working class and poor white people exchange the possibility of a multiracial democratic society, a society in which resources and power are shared in far more just and equitable ways, for the "white right" to feel superior. Over time, as white working people have fought for greater inclusion and economic justice, the ruling class has granted an expansion of white privileges economically, politically, and socially—once again, in exchange for suppressing the power of working class communities of color. A great synopsis of Du Bois's thinking can be found in Joel Olson's book Abolition Democracy.

My work focuses on political education, leadership development, and organizational support for white social justice effort and my work incorporates this understanding of white supremacy, white privilege, and racial oppression. This is done, not so we can just be less racist or more aware, but so we can be more effective building the kind of grassroots movements we need to bring down white supremacy and structural inequality.

Far too often, conversations about white privilege just talk about racism that communities of color experience, and then white privilege that white communities experience, and then give white people the impression that what is needed is for more and more white people to be aware of privilege and act against racism. These are good things, and they can be helpful places to start, but it leaves out power, and by that I mean ruling class power and structural power/injustice.

When you leave out challenging the structures of power, then our work against racism and white privilege can very quickly become focused on individual behavior. Without a power analysis, then it can become just about raising awareness, without the larger goal of making structural change. Structural change requires building move-

Dardanelle, AR population 4600. Photo: Meredith Martin-Moates

ments of millions of people. And for me, the process of working against injustice and for liberation is where the seeds of the new society begin to flourish. Social **change** movements nurture and give rise to cultures of solidarity, cultures fused with liberation values. Cultures and values of liberation put into practice through grassroots people's movements is where we see profound changes in our lives, families, communities, and institutions.

To put it another way, we can't think our way out of the problem of white privilege by being really aware white people. We need to be aware white people on our own personal growth journey, who want to bring large numbers of other white people into movements to bring down white supremacy and build up multiracial democracy and a socialist economy. So we need to talk about white privilege with that orientation—which means sometimes not using the term white privilege directly at all, but conveying the ideas behind it through language that will resonate with people.

Katy: Have you experienced pushback on the phrase from other white people? How do you respond? What are some common ways the phrase is called into question, and how do you address those?

Chris: How I respond really depends on who the person is and where they are politically. For example, as a young person I would go head to head with right-wing people in my family and it was exhausting. Then I realized that if my goal was to get my rightwing Grandpa to become an anti-racist, feminist, socialist, then I was setting myself up or failure and I wasn't going to be spending my time and energy wisely. So with my Grandpa, my goal became, how to make him a less effective racist, sexist, homophobe, and so on. Which meant rather than debate him at Thanksgiving and give him a platform that he commanded, I tried to use humor to disarm him and then put out ideas about white privilege and racism—not to convince him—but to engage other people in my family who routinely remained silent in those conversations. I asked people in my family who I knew had different, more progressive values, to share what they thought. I tried to open space for other voices, and understood that debates with my Grandpa were for me to develop my own thinking rather than change his.

But often times people come to me and want to know how they can convince someone in their family who they love, but who they doggedly oppose politically. My response is this is that we need to spend less time trying to move people who aren't moveable and focus our energies on people around us who, in moments like the uprising in Ferguson, are actually moveable. People around us who are asking questions, who

Dardanelle, AR. Photo Meredith Martin-Moates

17

are open to learning more, who might want to do to a demonstration but have never done anything like that before. Often we focus a lot of energy on jackasses and trolls; [meanwhile,] the people who are closer to us politically, but don't know how to get involved, are ignored. That said, in public debates or classroom conversations, it is important to challenge such voices, but, again, from the perspective that the people you're really trying to move are the folks listening, not the jackass who denies that race is a factor in Ferguson.

> **❝ We need to be aware white people on our own personal growth journey, who want to bring large numbers of other white people into movements to bring down white supremacy...❞**

We need to get really good at seeing opportunities for white people to get involved in and/or support racial justice efforts and ask people, directly, to step into those opportunities. When people are in motion working for social justice, they go to meetings, a rally, a cultural event, or join an organization. They learn and grow at a much quicker pace than when they are just engaged in discussion or study. Going back to the term white privilege...When white people participate in multiracial social justice activities and hear people of color talk about racism and their experiences, significant shifts will take place. It becomes less of an academic conversation and becomes rooted in people's lives and experiences.

That said, we still need to have a lot of conversations with white people. In my talks and writing about racism directed towards white people, I regularly speak from my own experience of coming to consciousness about racism, white privilege, and how devastating and painful it was. I do this because white people often feel defensive in conversations about race. The focus becomes "proving I'm not a racist" rather than trying to understand what racism is and how we can end it. I know that, because I have so often felt that defensiveness. So often when white people become conscious about racism and their own white privilege, they hate themselves and project that hate onto hating other white people. I remember a mentor of mine, an organizer of color, who said, "I understand why you would have animosity towards other white people, but you need to learn how to organize them." Later, I read a great quote from legendary white anti-racist organizer Anne Braden, who said "You can't organize people you hate." So, you need to work though a lot of the emotions that come up as we become aware and get active. This comes in time, through experience. But the main thing is that we need to have our eyes on the prize of why we're having these conversations, what we're trying to accomplish, and work to be able to speak to other people who have the same privileges as us, from a place of love and from a place of "we need movements of millions playing many different roles, to bring down these systems of oppression that pit us against each other and maintain unthinkable violence."

Katy: Why do you feel it's a vital phrase to use?

Chris: I think it communicates a lot about the way white people individually and collectively fit into the structures of white supremacy. And at this point, conversations about white privilege are happening all over the place, in ways that it's hard to believe looking back 25 years ago. This is a good thing. And again, we need to use the concept to help us all get free. And this comes back to this concept of collective liberation and, for me, one of my goals is to help white people find their self-interest in dismantling white supremacy, and for men to understand how their lives can be profoundly improved through challenging patriarchy—not to stop there, but to include this part about how systems of oppression also negatively impact the people who are privileged. Going back to Du Bois, he was clear that white working class and poor people had far more to gain by joining with working class and poor people of color to fight for a better world. My friend Terence explained it to me this way. He told me that one of the ways that racism hurt me (jarring to hear a Black person tell me that I was hurt by racism) was by teaching me that I have nothing to learn from the histories, cultures, social justice movements, visions, and lives of communities of color. As a social justice activist, I was being denied the powerful insights and inspirations from people of color-led movements which have been at the heart of social justice efforts in this country.

I bring that perspective with me. I don't have conversations with white people to make them feel guilty about having white privilege. I talk about white privilege as one of the ways that institutional racism is maintained, and that all of our hopes for a better world rest squarely on building powerful multiracial movements to solve the most pressing problems of our times. I press that white people have to make a choice between which side of history they want to be on: The history of slavery, genocide, and lynching, or the history of people coming together to create what Anne Braden called the "Other America"—the America of multiracial democracy and equality for all people, the America of the Abolitionists, the Freedom Riders, and the Dream

Defenders. I try to follow that up with how people can get involved.

I'll share one other story about how we have to listen deeper rather than just use the right words. Words are important and they matter, but we also need to listen to people's hearts and souls. A white working class friend of mine was the first person to go to college in her family. She learned about the history of white supremacy and white privilege in a class and was enraged. One day, she came home from school and started a conversation about immigration with her mom. Her mom said, "It's a shame about all those illegals being deported." My friend jumped all over her mom for using the word illegal and only later realized her mom was expressing sympathy that could have then be explored and potentially developed into solidarity. Our goal is to move white people towards a collective liberation vision and strategy of solidarity and unity.

> "Our goal is to move white people towards a collective liberation vision and strategy of solidarity and unity."

Maybe the person is ready to talk about white privilege, or maybe they first just need to understand that racism exists. Start with where people are at and move them where you can. Prioritize who you're investing time and energy into. Helping get 15 white people to take a stand in your small town, rural area, or suburb and demonstrating in solidarity with the kids from Central America crossing the border, or showing solidarity with Ferguson, can have a bigger impact than arguing on Facebook or in person with reactionary family members and friends for hours. Get a demonstration like that together and invite folks to attend it who you're not sure about as far as where they stand on an issue. One of our roles, as white anti-racists, is to give more and more white people opportunities to stand on the right side of history.

Katy: Are there any resources or links you would recommend to a white person newly acquainting themselves with the idea of white privilege? Any other links on the subject for the world at large?

Chris: I think taking a moment to think about the person you're trying to reach and think about what they would be interested in, what would speak to them and appeal to them. So maybe it's a book focused on structural inequality or the history of racism in the U.S. Or maybe it's a novel by Toni Morrison or poems by June Jordan or essays by bell hooks or Audre Lorde. Or maybe it's watching a movie like American History X or a documentary like Shakti Butler's Mirrors of Privilege: Making Whiteness Visible, and having a conversation afterwards.

Public School Teachers Organizing in North Carolina. Photo: Bryan Profitt

For two pretty accessible beginning-to-think-about-these-issues books, I would recommend Paul Kivel's Uprooting Racism: How White People Can Work for Racial Justice and Beverly Daniel Tatum's "Why Are All the Black Kids Sitting Together in the Cafeteria?" And Other Conversations About Race.

The one thing I'd say to keep in mind is to try as often as you can to let white people in your life know that there have been white anti-racists throughout history who have made important contributions and who they can learn about. It's important to give people hope and suggestions for next steps to keep moving.

....

Katy Otto *is a writer, musician, and social justice activist, originally from the D.C. area, now living and working in Philadelphia. She plays drums in "Trophy Wife" and "Callowhill," runs the independent label Exotic Fever Records, and writes for Feministing, The Media, Role Reboot, and other outlets. She is passionate about social justice—from reproductive health access to racial justice to animal rights.*

Anti-Black Racism, the Minstrel Show, and the Making of Whiteness

Mike Brown Silent Protest at the White House, Washington D.C. Photo: Elvert Barnes

For all of us who want to move white people into anti-racist consciousness and actions, we must remember the dual role that anti-Black racism plays in disciplining white people to capitalist exploitation. Anti-Black racism was most famously fused into popular culture and ideology through the Blackface minstrel shows. The minstrel show became the national art form by the mid-1800s, and taught millions of Europeans, many of them recent immigrants, what it meant to be white. In fact, the term "Jim Crow," used to describe the segregated apartheid South after Reconstruction, comes from a highly popular character, in black face, in the early days of the minstrel show.

On the one hand, the minstrel shows were intended to discipline immigrant Europeans, from a wide range of agriculture-based cultures, into the White Protestant work ethic that barons of industry wanted infused in their workforce. Industrial capitalism wanted a workforce that internalized the values of a self-sacrificing work ethic and a culture of individualism. Industrial capitalism devastated European-American workers' sense of community, and sense of self as bosses looked for ever more ways to exploit workers' labor to make profits. This was a time of expanding slums, growing alcoholism, and, to fight back, workers beginning to form unions.

On the surface, the minstrel show is about Black culture. Black culture was portrayed as promoting laziness (lacking a Protestant work ethic), with Black people exhibiting the playfulness of children and the lustfulness of beasts (totally lacking the values of self-sacrifice and self-mastery). Below the surface, the minstrel show was teaching European-Americans what it meant to be white in a capitalist economy. Being white meant you were supposed to be a self-made man (or married to one), exercise self-control, work hard, not rock the boat, and pull your weight (i.e., make bosses rich, not complain about wages or work conditions). Being a white man meant protecting white women from the uncontrollable lust of the Black man.

The minstrel show taught European-Americans that to be white meant despising the supposedly "incompetent" and "lazy" culture of Black people that makes them forever dependent on white people to take care of them. In the minstrel show, white people are civilized and Black people are borderline animals who either need to be taken care of for their own good, or are dangerous beasts out to get white women.

The underlying themes of the minstrel show are all around us today. Everyone must pull themselves up by their own bootstraps and if you aren't economically prosperous, well then, you have no one to blame but yourself. White people are told they are superior to all others, and so if you are white and not wealthy, then it must be because those dependent, lazy, childlike Blacks and other people of color are pulling you and the economy down. Or, Blacks and other people of color are cheats and criminals, both common minstrel show characters, who are stealing from white America directly or have pulled a con and are stealing from white America collectively—through welfare, food stamps, or by taking unionized public sector jobs or spots in college away from more qualified whites through Affirmative Action. None of this is true, of course, but white supremacy isn't about truth. White supremacy in the United States is primarily about organizing the economy and the political system to serve the interests of elites at the expense of the vast majority of people. White supremacy is a divide-and-rule strategy to maintain structural inequality and the logic and culture of supremacy systems that normalize and rationalize inequality.

James Baldwin famously said to white America, "If I am not who you think I am, you are not who you think you are." Our responsibility as white anti-racists who want to dismantle white supremacy, who want to win and build a world where Black lives matter, who want economic justice for all, our responsibility is to understand that white racist rage and white resistance to Black equality is rooted in white anger and pain for not achieving the American Dream. Working class and poor white people, and even more and more white middle class people, are experiencing the long-term effects of stagnant wages while CEOs make millions and TV shows make it seem like everyone is bringing in $150,000 a year (even middle class Blacks).

With decades of right-wing-led cuts to public institutions like schools, libraries, and parks, alongside massive spending to expand policing and the prison system, many white people are told that society is both out of control and that the pathologically dependent and criminal culture of Black and Brown America is to blame. White people have been sold a pack of lies about working hard and achieving economic prosperity. When that prosperity doesn't happen, it isn't the fault of multinational corporations that moved decent paying union jobs out of the U.S. to exploit third world workers, and it isn't the fault of the Republican and Democratic Parties that have passed legislation funneling money to corporate power; it's because of Brown-skinned immigrants and dark-skinned welfare families.

Recently, I was at an immigrant rights demonstration in Nashville, Tennessee. President Obama was visiting an immigrant social service provider and there were dueling protests. There were those, like myself, who wanted Obama to pass far-reaching immigration reform based in economic justice for all and multiracial democracy rather than criminalization. Then there were the Tea Party anti-immigrant protesters calling from mass deportation and further militarization of the Border. I was standing next to a working class white mother, holding her young child in one hand and an anti-immigrant sign in the other. She told me she was protesting Obama because he was letting "illegal" immigrants stay in the country and get food stamps, while she herself had been denied food stamps to take care of her kids. Most of the white Tea Party people there were middle class, and I felt quite confident that most or all of them had been fighting to have food stamps cut. While the majority demographic utilizing welfare and food stamps is white people, the rhetoric used is that it's Black and Brown women who are taking advantage of the system and eating lobster, while hard-working stiffs can barely afford to put food on their families' plates.

> **"This is the process of embracing our shared humanity, creating a just world and building beloved community."**

I was holding my son at that rally as well. In the mother's words, I felt the pain and tragedy of anti-Black racism in white lives, as well as its ability to marshal violent political racist action. I looked at our children, both being raised white in a culture still teaching the values performed in the minstrel show, and I felt the tremendous need to save our kids from the death culture of white supremacy.

For white anti-racists, our task is to demand that Black lives matter and learn to deeply speak to, bear witness to, and listen to the pain underneath white racist rage and resentment. We must learn how to listen to white racial pain and attach it to the real enemy of structural inequality and name racism as the violent poison that it is.

Our task is to simultaneously work in solidarity with Black leadership and people of color building this movement, and to develop the leadership of white anti-racists, particularly working class and poor people's leadership. Our vision is both a world where Black lives matter and a society based on multiracial democracy and economic justice for all, where the hearts and minds of white people have been freed from the death culture of white supremacy and anti-black racism.

As people racialized as white in a white supremacist society, we must forge new identities rooted in liberation values, and committed to challenging structural oppression. This is the process of unlearning the lies of capitalist individualism and racist fear. This is the process of embracing our shared humanity, creating a just world and building beloved community. When we break white silence that gives consent to racism, we must speak fluently and courageously about a life-affirming culture and society that also uproots capitalism and builds economic justice for all.

Occupation of Capitol, Madison, WI. Photo: Leslie Amsterdam Peterson

For Michael Brown and Ferguson: Facing White Fears of Blackness and Taking Action to End White Supremacy

The police murder of Michael Brown and the courageous resistance of his family and the Black community in Ferguson, Missouri, have once again brought the attention of the country to the devastating reality of racist violence, structural inequality, and the need for Black communities to demand that "Black Lives Matter." With outrage, grief, and pain all over the country, I'm writing this to white people in particular as a call to action to stand with the people of Ferguson and to work against racism. Below are nine suggestions for moving into action and challenging racism. But first, let's be honest with each other. White fear of Blackness isn't just something that racist extremists experience; it's a core part of white consciousness and how structural violence and inequality are maintained.

I remember a few years ago, opening my front door and seeing five unfamiliar Black teenage boys on and around my front porch. With my baby in my arm, my initial

Little Rock, AR Collective Liberation Study Group.
Photo: Meredith Martin-Moates

reaction was fear. Fear that these teenage boys would re-enact countless scenes of racialized crime and violence that I've consumed since I was a little kid. It's not the kind of experience someone who has been doing anti-racist work for twenty-five years likes to admit having, but this isn't a time for false pretenses to protect our egos. This is a time for white people to recognize that our irrational fears of Blackness are the result of the logic of white supremacy, which is intended to concentrate power into the hands of the few by creating and maintaining structural violence and inequality.

Throughout my life, I have routinely experienced fear of Blackness, particularly working class and poor Black men, as it has been intimately and relentlessly weaved into my subconscious through images, everywhere, of dark-skinned people doing bad things to light-skinned people, and in my consciousness through political, economic, and cultural attacks, everywhere, on Black communities. For a long time I felt guilty for having these feelings, and they demobilized me. But over time I began to recognize the roots of these fears and I tapped into my rage against the white supremacist society that raised me and rewards me for having them, and that rage has helped mobilize me.

When I experience these irrational fears, I remind myself that this is the legacy of slavery, of Jim Crow apartheid, of anti-Black racism used to justify economic exploitation and social violence, that these fears are one of the ways that white supremacy lives in my body and subconsciously works to organize my life by dividing me from Black people and supporting (actively or through indifference) their subjugation, and uniting me to ruling class agendas of concentrating wealth and power through structural violence and inequality.

I also remind myself of who has actually, historically, been the target of race-based violence. I think of the power of multiracial justice organizing and community in my life, and how racism actively works to destroy such community and how grateful I am to all who throughout history have worked to create another way for us to be together. And, finally, I think about how poisonous these racist fears and hatreds are, how they generated guilt and shame in my life as I worked to become a social justice activist, and the damage and pain they create in the lives of the people I love, all around me.

And I let all of this converge in my body, to feel the emotional roots of why I am committed to collective efforts to ending the horrors of white supremacy in all of our lives.

The struggle to liberate our minds and bodies is vital and it must be part of larger collective efforts to confront existing unjust power and create structural equality and justice for all people. Here are nine suggestions to help move forward.

1. Demonstrate Our Outrage and Demand Change. In whatever way you can, make your opposition to these police murders of Black people known. Look to see if there are demonstrations organized by Black-led and people of color-led groups that you can participate in and recruit people to join. Support these efforts in whatever way you can. If such demonstrations are not taking place, reach out to people in your life and help create public expressions of outrage, protest, and grief with a central message that Black Lives Matter, these murders must end, and we are opposed to racism.

In rural areas, towns, suburbs, and cities in every region of the country, we must act with the people in Ferguson and with Black communities around the country protesting the racist murders in their communities. Every 28 hours a Black person is murdered by police, security guards, or white (or non-Black) people who declare they were protecting themselves from Black people. Demonstrations are an opportunity to move people in our lives to take a stand, and to build relationships with people and organizations in our communities.

2. Grieve and Love Publicly and Privately. Connect to the pain of this moment and be with the pain that is all around us in our families and communities. Often we skip grieving and go to action, but grieving can connect us to a deeper power within us, and connect us to each other. Capitalism wants us to detach from our emotions, to detach from ourselves and the impacts we have on each other and the world. Liberation is a process of re-attachment to our humanity, the humanity of others, the earth, and the sacredness of life. Love others as they grieve—be present, be supportive, and find strength in our relationships with one another. Try not to fear grief, as there is power in our collective and personal grief. Fear the numbing of structural violence and inequality that robs us of the power of love in the face of the death culture we live in.

3. Awaken and Change Hearts and Minds. The protests in Ferguson and the pleas from loved ones of Michael Brown, particularly his mother, have created a national focus on the epidemic of police murders of Black people. This focus can shine a light on white supremacy and the everyday racism of our society. This is a moment when people, white people in particularly, are searching to make sense of what is happening. This is a moment when we can work for mass conversion, to raise consciousness, to awaken people in our lives and networks to the brutal dehumanizing reality of injustice, as well as the possibilities of working for systemic equality. Do not be afraid of speaking truth with courage—take small steps, celebrate small victories, and build your confidence to do more.

4. Get Connected and Throw Down. Work on and support Black-led and people of color-led justice campaigns nationally and locally. Get involved in struggles to win changes and use those campaigns to get more and more of the people in your life involved. Get involved in whatever works for your life. All of what we do matters, when we do it together with a goal and vision of where we are going. Get started with ColorofChange.org, NotOne-MoreDeportation.com, and Jobs with Justice (jwj.org).

5. Bridges Not Divisions. The divisions of race, class, and gender play out in society and in our work for change. This is to be expected, so we must do all we can to prepare ourselves to overcome these divisions. Anti-racism, feminism, class consciousness, and disability justice can all help us create powerful solidarities, communities, , and movements to change society.

6. Build Liberation Culture Rooted in People's History. Help create cultures of solidarity and love between our communities and different struggles. Everyday, in profound and subtle ways we are torn apart from each other and told we are powerless. This self-defeating narrative in the minds of everyday people is critical for rulers to maintain power. We must tune in to the long traditions of narratives of mutuality, empowerment, and collective liberation, particularly in communities of color and working class communities. We must learn about and celebrate the stories of everyday people coming together, and share our own stories with our communities.

7. Set Goals to Help Us All Get Free. Set goals for your work for justice, for your personal growth, and for your efforts to create cultures of solidarity and love. Find what motivates you to take action, and remember that we are in this for the long haul.

8. Study to Decolonize Your Mind and Reclaim Your Heart. Take time to read and study those who have gone before us; learn the lessons from their efforts. Root yourself in the history of people's movements for justice and equality. Read analysis to help make sense of the economic and political system and how exploited labor, white supremacy, patriarchy, homophobia, and ableism are central to the structural violence and inequality in our society. Learn about the visionary change others envision and develop your own vision. Get started with the zinnedproject.org, and go further with Vincent Harding's There Is a River: The Black Struggle for Freedom in America, Barbara Ransby's Ella Baker and the Black Freedom Struggle, and Catherine Fosl's Subversive Southerner: Anne Braden and the Struggle for Racial Justice in the Cold War South.

9. Be Powerful and Strive to Get Free. Develop your abilities through personal and collective efforts to be as powerful, effective, healthy, and whole as you can be. We need people who are fully alive to win and create the change we need. Remember that we grow in powerful ways through collective action for justice. Our trust in ourselves and in each other grows as we challenge illegitimate authority and realize the power we have together in creating a democratic society with equality and justice, truly, for all people. We are more brilliant, strategic, visionary, and effective than we know, when we believe in each other and ourselves, and take action together.

For Michael Brown, Eric Garner, Renisha McBride, Trayvon Martin, and so many more and all their families. For Black children around the country who grow up in the shadow of socially sanctioned racist violence. For white children and all non-Black children who are being raised to fear and hate Blackness and detach from their humanity in the process. Let us be courageous in the face of this violently racist society. Let us draw strength from past people's movements and join with others today to end racism, work for racial justice, and create a much better world for all of our children and young people. Let us move beyond fear and guilt and cultivate our love and rage.

Door Knocking for BLM and Giving Out Lawnsigns, Austin, TX .
Photo: Roan Boucher

For a Theology of Liberation: An interview with Rev. Ashley Horan of the Minnesota Unitarian Universalist Social Justice Alliance

Shortly after addressing a packed room of over 400 mostly white faith activists from around the country at the Unitarian Universalist Selma 50th Anniversary Commemoration Conference in Alabama, Opal Tometi, one of the co-founders of Black Lives Matter and someone I worked alongside fighting the "Show Me Your Papers" anti-immigrant legislation in Arizona, gave me a quick look and said, "We need to build up the anti-racist work with white people, to meet the enormous needs in these times," in between conversations she had with a dozen people waiting to talk with her.

It wasn't a new message or a call for work I wasn't already doing. The difference this time is that we are living in a time of Black liberation "on-the-move." Racist structural violence is in the headlines and national debate in a way I've never experienced as a 41-year-old Gen Xer who came of racial consciousness with the Rodney King uprising in Los Angeles in 1992.

With tens of thousands of white people coming into consciousness and thousands of experienced white anti-racists trying to figure out how to step up, this interview with Unitarian Universalist leader Rev. Ashley Horan, and this series of interviews with white racial justice leaders and organizers around the country who are engaging and moving white communities, is one of my efforts

Die-in at Mall of the America, Twin Cities, MN.
Photo: Ashley Horan

to meet the need my comrade Opal Tometi and so many others have made plain. I want to provide concrete examples of what anti-racist values and politics look like in practice. How do we raise consciousness and move white people into action for racial justice? How do white anti-racists form powerful multiracial alliances? How can white people step up and bring leadership in these Black Lives Matter times? These are the questions that have driven my work over the past two decades and these are the questions I explore throughout the interviews collected in this book.

I first came into my own Unitarian Universalist faith when I was brought in as a member of Catalyst Project to lead anti-racist organizing trainings for hundreds of fired up, passionate UU youth from around the U.S. and Canada. Mostly white, with a strong crew of young people and adults of color, a strong commitment to anti-racism and social justice, a faith based in the interconnectedness of all life and the inherent worth and dignity of all people, I was ready to sign up. The UUs met a spiritual need in my life, and as an anti-racist organizer, I also saw the tremendous potential of hundreds of thousands of mostly white people, with a small, but powerful and growing, people of color membership, in a denomination with a formal commitment to anti-racism, as well as visionary and strong leadership for radicals of color and radical white anti-racists, even when embattled with institutional resistance and a slower pace of change then they'd like, along with a significantly feminist, queer, anti-racist, anti-capitalist youth and young adult movement raising new generations of movement builders.

Reverend Ashley Horan is one of those younger adults who is leading the Unitarian Universalist faith towards the anti-racist, multiracial, multicultural, welcoming denomination it strives to be, along with the UU church being a powerful force for collective liberation in the world. And in these Black liberation movement times, she is organizing UUs in Minnesota to show up for Black Lives Matter, and in the process is inspiring other white UUs to do the same around the country. This interview lifts up faith-based work as a lens to help all of us think about calling forward our values and beliefs in the service of justice and to move people through their congregations and spirituality.

Chris Crass: How are you working to move white people into the racial justice movement in this time? What's working? And what are you learning from what works?

Ashley Horan: I am a Unitarian Universalist minister, currently serving as the Executive Director of MUUSJA, the Minnesota Unitarian Universalist Social Justice Alliance, which is our statewide justice and advocacy network. We bring together Unitarian Universalists from around the state to both build power and serve as a public moral voice for our faith in issue-based organizing, and develop the capacity of our congregations to do effective, accountable social justice work in their local areas. Historically, we have focused on issues such as LGBTQIA (Lesbian, Gay, Bisexual, Transsexual, Queer, Intersex, Asexual) rights, housing/homelessness, health care, environmental justice, voting rights, and racial justice.

These past few months, we have been supporting the groundswell of vibrant, visionary organizing being done by the leaders of Black Lives Matter Minneapolis, as a part of our ongoing commitment to racial justice. MUUSJA members—who are also almost always members and clergy of local Unitarian Universalist congregations—participated in force at the Mall of America protest in December, as well as many public protests, marches, educational events, and trainings that have been put on by the BLM folks over the past number of months.

> **"...our faith calls us to this work of solidarity, and uprooting white supremacy..."**

On an organizational level, as the director of a small faith-based nonprofit, I don't have a huge number of resources—but I am doing my best to do what the mantra that hangs in my office says: "Do what you can, where you are, with what you have." For me in my current context, that means entering into conversations with the Board of Trustees of my organization to develop a shared consensus that we support the work of Black Lives Matter Minneapolis (who are doing some seriously fierce organizing here in the Twin Cities!). While we are still developing a shared sense of what "supporting the work" looks like, they are on board with us using the resources we have to get the message out—which means publicizing Black Lives Matter actions and opportunities for engagement, developing talking points for people of our faith tradition to talk from a theologically grounded place about why our faith calls us to this work of solidarity, and uprooting white supremacy, using our social media and email lists to amplify the reach of BLM announcements to folks who might otherwise not see them, etc.

We have also intentionally sponsored events—like having Chris Crass here to speak!—that highlight the intersections of racial justice and other "issues" we're working on, such as LGBTQIA rights, environmental justice, healthcare, voting rights, etc. For me, making sure that I/we take advantage of every opportunity we can to highlight intersectionality is essential—it helps people strengthen the muscles they have for analysis and awareness, and brings people who have been siloed in their own "issue areas" into conversation with the broader Movement.

"we are all born with inherent worth and dignity, from a wellspring of Love that desires our interdependence."

I also regularly show up myself, in a clerical collar, at all the local BLM events and identify myself by my title and organization whenever speaking to the media or folks who ask about where I serve. Showing up in "uniform," and speaking in my role as ED of a faith-based nonprofit, are intentional choices for me—not to draw focus away from anyone else, but to prompt people to think about "unexpected" people acting publicly as allies for racial justice. My appearance is often intriguing to people—young, queer, femme, fat, religious, white, often with a baby on my hip—largely because I am visibly embodying things that are contradictory to many people's expectations of both what a religious leader is and what a racial justice ally looks like.

What I'm learning from all of this in working with white people is that curiosity is a powerful motivator of connections, and that the stance we must take is an invitational one—not a strident, shaming, zealous one. When we have the latter posture, it's too easy for white people to say, "Racial justice and anti-racism are somebody else's issue, not mine." But when we walk in the world in a way that allows people to enter into our personal stories, to ask us questions, to come closer, to see how they might also see racism and white supremacy as separating them from wholeness and health that they yearn for... People are willing to lean in and risk learning more.

Rally in Minneapolis, MN. Photo by Ashley Horan

Chris: How do you think about effectiveness and how do you measure it? Can you share an experience that helps you think about effective work in white communities for racial justice?

Ashley: I think about effectiveness not so much in terms of quantifiable statistics (although I do like to think about white people's money moving to people of color-led organizing for liberation!), but in terms of the stories white people tell about their worlds opening up. I think about people waking up to the reality that whiteness is not "the norm" for everything; beginning to develop authentic relationships with people

"My goal is to get the people I serve to be able to articulate a theology of salvation by interconnection."

who don't live in their neighborhoods or go to their churches; intentionally seeking out commentary and news and writing and film and art made by people of color; stepping out of their comfort zones and into action when they are called to act as allies by people with whom they have been deepening their connections. I think these stories ring true as successes to me because they signal a shift in the dominant paradigm—one that counts on white people both benefitting from and being completely oblivious to the extreme disparities and intentional, well-functioning structures that maintain white supremacy. And when white folks begin to narrate stories that reflect a growing consciousness rooted in both theoretical learning and real relationships, I believe we've "saved more souls" for the cause—souls who, once they awaken, begin to see themselves as servants of the Movement.

Chris: What are the goals and strategies (as emergent, planned, messy, and sophisticated—basic as they may be) you're operating from?

Ashley: As a religious leader of Unitarian Universalists, my goal is to get the people I serve to be able to articulate a theology of salvation by interconnection—one in which we are all born with inherent worth and dignity, from a wellspring of Love that desires our interdependence and health and has endowed us with the power to be agents of that salvation right here, right now, on this earth. In organizer language,

I'm trying to get people to understand collective liberation, and to sense both the blessing and the responsibility of claiming a belief that none of us is free until all of us are free.

The strategies all have to do with patient, long-term building of relationships—among individuals, congregations, and communities. Whether it's using a wide variety of communications media and tools to ensure that people of diverse ages and styles can stay connected with work that is happening, or creating worship designed to get people to turn toward one another and engage in deeper conversations, or inviting people to participate in political actions that they may never have felt bold enough to do before, the end goal is to get people to start conversations; to step out of their comfort zones; to begin to build relationships with people who look and live and believe differently than they do. Ultimately—and again, to use traditional religious language—I want to help as many people as possible, in as many ways as possible, feel "saved" by belonging to something larger than ourselves…something that both honors the realities of our different and unequal experiences in this world because of our identities, and points to the deeper commonalities and transcendent love that unite us.

I am achingly, profoundly aware that white supremacy is a metasystem that requires systemic solutions to dismantle. At the same time, though, we can never be organized enough to come up with a dismantling plan of attack if we don't have personal relationships with one another that are strong enough to hold us accountable and fiercely when $&*t hits the fan. I'll leave it to other people to come up with the blueprints for dismantling the system, and happily follow their lead; in the meantime, I feel called to developing as many interconnected people who are deeply committed to one another and to the salvific act of dismantling white supremacy as possible.

Chris: What challenges are you facing? How are you trying to overcome them? What are you learning from these experiences?

Ashley: Largely, right now, I'm working with mostly middle- to upper-middle class, educated white liberals. This means that most people are theoretically sympathetic to the work of combating white supremacy and creating a racially just and equitable world. So the resistance I see is more subtle, and it largely comes in two forms.

In the first, liberal white people use bureaucracy to throw up red tape where it doesn't need to exist. They ask whether there's a policy in place to allow the institution to focus on racial justice, or raise concerns about safety and fiduciary responsibility, or suggest that there are more emergent and pressing responsibilities that we need to address before we move into racial justice work. Liberals tend to be both somewhat anti-authoritarian and very deeply institutionalist, and this leads to pushing back against visionary leadership that demands a rewriting of the status quo, and spending a lot of energy making sure the institutions and structures in which they live and move do not undergo true transformation.

In the second, liberal white people assert that "racism isn't really the problem." Some say we should really be focusing on class and wealth inequality, some insist that if we don't address climate change first and foremost we'll all be underwater anyway. Name your issue, and white liberals have a thousand statistics and expert studies and arguments to back themselves up. But this tactic is a classic example of either/or thinking, and of the ways white culture encourages people to privilege "empirical data" and academic theories over the real, lived experiences of people who tell stories of a different kind of reality. And, in a lot of ways, I really understand this impulse—intersectionality is really difficult to wrap your mind around, and intersectional approaches to justice work take a very long time and are always messy.

I think there's a great deal of power in lovingly but directly naming these things when they happen. Usually, my tactic is to talk about how I've displayed the same kind of resistance at various moments, and how I've come to realize that this is one of the ways that white supremacy can be so sneaky in colonizing our minds—by making us think that Something Else That Liberals Should Care About is going on, and leading us to redirect our energy away from dismantling racism. This is one of the only times I ever think it's a good idea to triangulate: me, the person I'm talking to, and white supremacy. When I conspiratorially invite someone in by pointing out what a jerk white supremacy can be, we begin to build a relationship together and view white supremacy as our common enemy.

Chris: How are you developing your own leadership and the leadership of people around you to step up in these profound, painful, and powerful Black Lives Matter movement times?

Ashley: I'm reading a lot—intentionally seeking out writings about the strategies and realities being lived out by leaders of the BLM movement. Looking for alternative media that believes and privileges the voices of Black people. Reading the thinking of my white comrades and friends who are deeply invested in organizing other white folks, and engaging in the spiritual practice of endeavoring to be allies. I know that learning and reading are just a small part of growing my leadership, but the image I have about this kind of learning is that every article, every interview, every infographic I read helps push back the fog of white supremacy that is always threatening to colonize my mind, widening the circle of clarity in which I can stand to look around,

"I think my main technique for helping to develop other white people's leadership is to, quite simply, keep inviting people."

make connections, engage in the struggle. And, frequently, I share these readings via social media—always with a little bit of commentary or a question—in order to engage other people in dialogue. You can say what you want about Facebook, but I have found that some of the most profound learnings and breakthroughs I've had with people in my community have happened because of conversations sparked by a posting thread.

In addition to learning and thinking, I'm working on a few specific skills and disciplines for anti-racist leadership: in particular, (1) being vulnerable with people in my life about ways in which I've made mistakes or felt caught off guard or been heartbroken by something that has happened, and (2) actively combating the white tendency toward competition in anti-racism work, either in terms of seeking accolades for the things we do or competing with one another to be the best anti-racist in the room at the expense of relationship and love for other white people. These practices can take a hundred different forms, but they ultimately bring me away from guilt and annoyance and burnout, and toward affection and hope and solidarity with my own people.

I think my main technique for helping to develop other white people's leadership is to, quite simply, keep inviting people. Invite them to engage in a private dialogue when something hard happens publicly on social media. Invite them to show up for the protest or the meeting or the workshop. Invite them to read this article, or talk to me about why I think that thing. Invite them to volunteer to lead that chant or chair this group or make that policy decision.

Recently, I co-facilitated a curriculum called Beloved Conversations: Dialogues About Race and Ethnicity at one of our local congregations. Over several weeks, participants from a largely white Unitarian Universalist congregation, a largely Black nondenominational Christian congregation, and members of several community organizations gathered together to tell stories and explore the ways that race and racism have shaped our consciousnesses (in different ways), and have kept us from working together for collective liberation. I and the other facilitators consistently used examples in our facilitation about what was happening in the local Black Lives Matter movement, and kept pushing folks—especially white people, most of whom were Baby Boomers—to show up for these BLM events, and to be clear that this moment is a critical opening for white people to leverage our visibility and our power to uplift the agenda of Black-led movements for liberation.

I was never sure whether any of this sunk in for my fellow white people. Clearly, this was a group who was still standing in awe of the work of the Civil Rights Era, but I wasn't sure whether they envisioned themselves as being a part of today's movement for racial justice; whether they were ready to answer the call. But then, several weeks after the program ended, I began seeing their faces show up at public events. A man in his 60s showed up at the Hennepin County Courthouse on the morning of the pre-trial hearing for the 36 people being charged in conjunction with the Mall of America protests. A 17-year-old (one of the few youth in the group) was a part of a group of nearly 1,000 Twin Cities area students who walked out of their schools on May Day to support Black Lives Matter and the MOA 36. When I saw them both at these events, they both commented on how, without their participation in these dialogues, and without the invitation to attend, they wouldn't have come. But, nonetheless, here they were—and my guess is it will not be the last time for either of them!

It's incredible to me how many white people have never been invited to show up for racial justice—ever—which translates into a huge number of people who have basically tuned out to the issue. Invitations—especially personal ones—are incredibly powerful, and when the invitation is grounded in relationship and mutual respect, my experience is that people tend to say "yes." Maybe not the first time, or the second, but eventually—if you invite people often enough to come along as a partner in the work—many, many people will take you up on it.

....

Ashley Horan *is a Unitarian Universalist minister serving as the Executive Director of MUUSJA: The Minnesota Unitarian Universalist Social Justice Alliance. She feels deeply called to nurture the spiritual health of The Movement, which generally looks to her like spiritual people getting more politically grounded and political people getting more spiritually grounded. She lives with her beloved, the Rev. Karen Hutt, and their two children—Zi (14 years old) and Aspen Bell (5 months old)—in Minneapolis.*

To learn more about the Minnesota Unitarian Universalist Social Justice Alliance, go to www.muusja.org.

Ferguson and Resistance Against the Black Holocaust

The people fighting back in Ferguson are heroes who deserve our respect, gratitude, prayers, and acts of solidarity. The people of Ferguson who are fighting back, in many different ways, have forced the country to look into the face of the enduring reality of the Black holocaust that began with the first Africans kidnapped and sold into the slave system.

The choice everyone must make is whether or not we will be Hitler's "Good Germans" who tacitly gave their support to the Nazis and decried the "animalistic Jews" who fought back in Warsaw. Will we be the Slave Society's "Good Americans" who may have quietly and privately thought slavery was immoral, but spit venom decrying the "irrational" and "counter-productive actions" of Nat Turner and slave uprisings from the 1600s–1800s? Will we be the well-intentioned, and often unintentional, defenders of misogynistic violence who decry those who fight back when they are being assaulted?

The people fighting back in Ferguson are, right now, providing the greatest hope for winning and creating a society in which Black families and communities are no longer—routinely and devastatingly—subjugated to daily structural inequality in every sphere of life, appalling racist violence by the state and individuals, and the degradation of white condescension and indifference.

Will you stand with the people of Ferguson, by directing your pain and outrage at the real enemies (the Ferguson police department, and all levels of government backing them) and do all you can to support the fight for racial and economic justice? Or will you choose, through actions or in-actions, to continue the shameful history of those who have let evil reign and only condemn those who oppose it—because it isn't the right time or being done the right way?

The people of Ferguson did not create this crisis. Centuries of white supremacy, a police system that evolved out of the slave patrols, unchecked state violence against communities of color, mass incarceration of over two million people, epidemic poverty, and the murder of a teenage boy named Michael Brown created this crisis. The people of Ferguson have created hope and possibility, through their resistance against the nightmare of the Black holocaust, that another world is possible. Do you stand with them? Or do you give your support, well intentioned or unintentional as it may be, to the enduring reality of the Black holocaust?

Beyond Bad Apples: For a New Ecosystem of Collective Liberation

Policing in Baltimore, Ferguson, NYC, and around the country isn't broken. It works brutally and efficiently as designed. Police are highly effective in their purpose as the armed enforcers of an economy that exploits and robs poor and working class people—particularly communities of color—and a political system that extracts power from poor and working class communities, with communities of color hardest hit. The police are the internal army designed to further, enforce, and maintain a deeply unequal society. The police were never intended to respect, let alone protect, Black lives. Police are intended to maintain white supremacist capitalist patriarchy, period.

Black Lives Matter isn't about removing bad apples; it's about building a new ecosystem rooted in collective liberation, with Black liberation at the core. The Black Lives Matter movement is the leading edge in uniting us for a better world. For white people, our charge is to both throw down against white supremacy and to join with Black leadership to build up the world our children and elders deserve.

Chicago SURJ Street Team talking with people about BLM. Photo: Byron Durham

"The Black Lives Matter movement is the leading edge in uniting us for a better world."

Ending White Supremacy Is in Everyone's Interest:
An Interview with Meta Mendel-Reyes of Kentuckians for the Commonwealth

In this time of the Black Lives Matter movement, white anti-racists around the country are looking for ways to move more and more white people into effective action against racism and for structural equality for the long haul. Kentuckians for the Commonwealth have a history of bringing together working class communities of color and white working class communities united by a shared vision, multi-issue campaigns, and a culture of solidarity. They work across ruling class divisions of racism, with an eye on forging relationships and long-term alliances across those divisions.

Brittany Ferrell and Alexis Templeton of Millennial Activists United in Ferguson.
Photo: Meta Mendel-Reyes

They build grassroots working class power statewide, in rural and urban communities. Founded in 1981, they currently have close to 9000 members, and they work on environmental issues, voter re-enfranchisement of people convicted of felonies, and tax reform for economic justice. They have also been involved in the Black Lives Matter movement across the state of Kentucky, moving white people into racial justice consciousness and action.

This interview is with longtime organizer, and steering committee member of Kentuckians for the Commonwealth, Meta Mendel-Reyes.

Chris Crass: How are you working to move white people into the racial justice movement in this time? What's working? And what are you learning from what works?

Meta Mendel-Reyes: Although I am on the National Leadership team of Showing Up for Racial Justice (SURJ), I would like to focus here on my role as a leader in Kentuckians for the Commonwealth (KFTC), a statewide, multi-issue, social justice organization in Kentucky. Our state is not an obvious site for anti-racism work, except in so far as we have a lot of white people. The percentage of African Americans as part of the total population is about 8%, which itself is much higher than other people of color—although the number of Latinos is growing. When you consider that these folks are not dispersed equally across the state, but concentrated around Louisville, Lexington, and Covington, there are whole swaths of the state, especially Eastern Kentucky, that are almost entirely white. So the challenge for KFTC is to bring these different regions together, around a vision of racial justice that is in the interest of all Kentuckians.

KFTC is remarkably grassroots and organized into county chapters. Each chapter elects a representative to the Steering Committee—I'm the representative for Madison County. The steering committee makes decisions for the organization, such as the decision to affiliate with SURJ. What's distinctive about our approach to white anti-racism is the fact that it includes all our regions, not just the more urban ones. In contrast to the many scenes of police brutality that we have witnessed on a national level, Eastern Kentucky is rural, poor, and working class. As part of Appalachia, Eastern Kentuckians have been stereotyped as racist, ignorant, incestuous caricatures—distortions that have served the purpose of the exploitative industries. The area's rich history of resistance to these industries, particularly coal, is forgotten or ignored.

So, how do you build a white, anti-racist movement in such an unlikely place?

At this moment of red-hot activism, spurred by the revelations of blatant murders by the police, one response to the question may be simply, Why bother? Why shouldn't the white anti-racism struggle focus on the places where white supremacy is most visible: the urban neighborhoods where black lives matter least? I think that there are reasons for paying attention to the rural heartland, and that it is more than a bastion of white racism. In fact, the rural white anti-racist movement has something to teach its urban counterpart about struggling for racial justice at the heart of what Kentuckian bell hooks calls imperialist, white supremacist, capitalist patriarchy.

Chris: How do you think about effectiveness and how do you measure it? Can you share an experience that helps you think about effective work in white communities for racial justice?

Meta: I think effectiveness depends a lot on context; what looks like progress in rural Kentucky may look like stasis, or even movement backward, elsewhere. In Eastern Kentucky, relationship building is key to effectiveness, even if the result is not a conviction of a police officer for racially motivated murder or a Federal investigation of police practices. By relationship, I mean both deeper understanding across difference and the ability to take action together.

An experience that has moved the work forward in both senses is KFTC's campaign for the Restoration of Voting Rights. Many states limit the ability of former felons to vote. The extent of the limitation varies from state to state. On one end

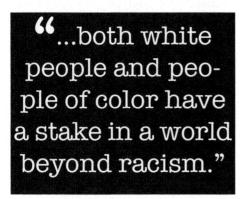

"...both white people and people of color have a stake in a world beyond racism."

of the spectrum is the right to vote while still in prison; at the opposite end is restriction of the vote until the penal process has been completed (being released from probation). Kentucky is the state that makes it the most difficult for former felons to reclaim the right to vote. In Kentucky, there is no automatic right to vote upon completion of your sentence and probation. Instead, you must apply to the Governor for what is essentially a pardon; there are no time limits, so the Governor can sit on

a request for as long as he wants or never grant the right to vote back. Those still waiting include a former naval officer who says that he can die for his country but cannot exercise the basic right of citizenship.

KFTC first became aware of the issue in African American neighborhoods of Louisville. However, we quickly found that the problem affected white Kentuckians too. As a result, an unlikely alliance was formed including urban African Americans and rural, white Eastern Kentuckians. Former felons and other KFTC members marched up the steps of the Capitol, rallying together and lobbying their representatives together. Both participated in events called "Singing for Democracy"; gospel voices from both religious traditions rang out over big city and small town. Yet restoration of voting rights is still a dream. For the last ten years, the bill to restore voting rights has passed in one House of the legislature, but has been stalled by a powerful Committee Chair in the State Senate.

If you measure effectiveness solely in terms of the passage of a law, then the campaign for the Restoration of Voting Rights is a failure. But if you look at the new relationships that have been built, and the actions taken together, then the campaign has been effective in moving the anti-racism movement forward.

Chris: What are the goals and strategies (as emergent, planned, messy, and sophisticated, basic as they may be) you're operating from?

Meta: The main goal is also a strategy: mutual interest. We feel strongly that we're not here to "help the downtrodden," which is condescending and reproduces relations of dependency. Instead, KFTC is about empowering people to move beyond the status of victims to a place where they are in charge of their own liberation. This is the opposite of dependency because the individual and the organization are on the same footing, working together for their mutual liberation. As the Aboriginal saying has

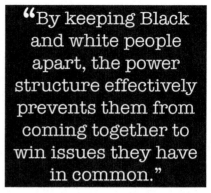

"By keeping Black and white people apart, the power structure effectively prevents them from coming together to win issues they have in common."

it, "If you've come to help me, no thank you, but if your liberation is bound up with mine, then come, let us work together."

In terms of race, this means that both white people and people of color have a stake in a world beyond racism. The price that people of color pay under the current system is obvious. The criminal "justice" system hinges on the school-to-prison pipeline; in fact, you could argue that the police murders just speed up the process, with so many young Black men killed before they even receive the facade of criminal justice.

But there are also costs that white people pay for participating in a system of white supremacy. Some of these are hard to quantify, such as the loss of true friendships across racial lines. But others can be counted in dollars and cents. By keeping Black and white people apart, the power structure effectively prevents them from coming together to win issues they have in common. Most Black and white people in

KFTC Annual Meeting. Photo: Meta Mendel-Reyes

Kentucky are working class, and could be uniting for fair wages, a fair tax code, and a healthy environment. Instead they blame each other, to the satisfaction of the capitalist forces that have a real stake in maintaining white supremacy.

One strategy that KFTC has used to bring people together in a common struggle is tax reform. In Kentucky's arcane tax structure, the lowest bracket pays a higher percentage of their income than does the wealthiest, along with other abuses. This cuts across lines of race, and KFTC has been successful in bringing Blacks and whites together to fight for economic justice. As with many things in Kentucky, success has to be qualified; due to the intransigence of the State Legislature, it is very hard to pass reform legislation. Yet, once again, relationships have been strengthened, in readiness for the next stage of the struggle.

Chris: What challenges are you facing? How are you trying to overcome them? What are you learning from these experiences?

KFTC members rally in Berea, KY.
Photo: Meta Mendel-Reyes

Meta: My effectiveness is limited because I am an outsider; although I have lived in here for 15 years, I will never be considered a Kentuckian. How can I work effectively with people whose stories are very different from mine—and is it right to even try? Regardless of doubts, I continue to do the slow work of relationship building, always bearing in mind that these are not my mountains, not my family stories of resistance. A key factor here is the value of mutual interest, my conviction that ending white supremacy is in the interest of all Kentuckians—white or Black, urban or rural, new or native.

A related challenge is the devastating power of white supremacy to warp Appalachian Kentuckians' recognition of their own interest in racial justice. As suggested above, the extractive industries and their governmental toadies have been very successful in using race as a wedge to divide and conquer those who could otherwise use their unified power for change. As a result, many rural whites stare at their televisions, identifying not with the victims of police brutality, but with the owners of damaged property or with the police themselves. Buried beneath these manipulative tactics is the history of struggle against industries and agencies that could help people recog-

nize "which side [they are] on." Reclaiming that history is an impor
reclaiming their stolen identities, as people in struggle.

On the personal side, I struggle with hopelessness and self-doubt. It helps to recognize that these are forms of indulgence, to the extent that they provide excuses for sitting on the sideline. Yes, victory can seem impossible, and I may make mistakes, but that is when it is most important to pick myself up and re-enter the struggle. At these moments, the history of resistance mentioned above can be a powerful impetus for moving forward. In fact, this may be the Eastern Kentuckian gift to the white anti-racist movement: another **story of a people who refused to give in to force.**

Chris: How are you developing your own leadership and the leadership of people around you to step up in these profound, painful, and powerful Black Lives Matter movement times?

Meta: In terms of personal leadership, I try to surround myself with leaders. Both KFTC and SURJ are rich with experienced leaders who are wise, kind, and passionate. I have learned so much from the example of these folks as fighters but also as relationship builders. A small example is the way in which the SURJ Leadership Team checks in with each other at the beginning of every meeting, regardless of the length of the agenda. Both KFTC and SURJ take as long as possible to come to a difficult decision; in KFTC,

> **"...we get stronger as we reach out to others."**

we do take votes, but only rarely, and when we do, we make sure that all points of view have been heard.

The best leadership, I believe, goes hand in hand with alliance building; we get stronger as we reach out to others. Not that long ago, KFTC's Steering Committee met with leaders of the Climate Justice Alliance, in a small town in Eastern Kentucky. The groups had a lot in common, such as their work to end unjust environmental degradation that falls most heavily on the least powerful, and the search for a just transition that would move the Appalachian and the Southwestern economies beyond coal. But there was one difference, and finally one of our members named it: "Everybody on your side of the table is a person of color and everyone on our side is white!" That broke the ice, and for the rest of the weekend, Native Americans from Arizona and coal miners from Eastern Kentucky came together in a much deeper way than any of us would have thought possible. Through this kind of leadership, KFTC

.oes what it does best: bring people to take action together, across differences of race, state, and nation.

KFTC leaders have also taught me a great deal about developing leaders. I am particularly excited about the role of young people in KFTC, in SURJ, and in the Black Lives Matter movement. One thing that gives me hope is that, as in other rural areas, these young leaders in Eastern Kentucky have joined in the work to organize white people for racial justice. More and more, I see myself as an "Elder," available to pass on what I know, but not to claim that the way we did it is the only way to build a movement. Black Lives Matter is doing a great job of leading the struggle; I am proud to be a part of this movement that has reached all the way to Eastern Kentucky.

....

Meta Mendel-Reyes *is a member of the Leadership Team of Showing Up for Racial Justice (SURJ) and the Steering Committee of Kentuckians for the Commonwealth (KFTC). After years as an organizer with the United Farm Workers and other unions, she now teaches Peace and Social Justice Studies at Berea College in Kentucky.*

To learn more about Kentuckians for the Commonwealth, go to www.kftc.org.

Notes for White Anti-Racists Who Want to Build Movement for Black Liberation and Collective Liberation

I strongly encourage all of us working to move white people towards racial justice to have goals, take steps towards those goals, and evaluate and reassess both our goals and methods. Far too often in this work we just keep doing the same things over and over, expecting different results. For those of us who are white, we need to be careful that, in our rage and pain towards white supremacy and racist police violence, we don't look for fights with other white people as a way to "feel" like we are doing something. The adrenaline rush often followed by hopelessness is a dangerous cycle to be in, even if in the moment of the fight (often with the same handful of unmovable people) it feels like we are doing the right thing.

Black Liberation and White Anti-Racism panel with Alicia Garza, Robbie Clark, Phil Hutchings and Kamau Walton, Oakland, CA. Photo: Amanda Arkansassy Harris

One suggestion is that we as white folks be aware of when we are, as longtime reproductive justice organizer Loretta Ross says, "weaponizing" our analysis to attack other white people—as opposed to using it to fight institutional racism and trying to

Over 1000 people show up for panel organized by Catalyst Project.
Photo: Amanda Arkansassy Harris

bring other white people with us (not the ones firmly committed to upholding white supremacy, but the people around us who are often quiet in these conversations, on the sidelines, perhaps trying to make sense of what's going on, but don't know where to start—i.e., the people we need to be talking with, building with, and organizing, rather than wasting precious time and energy on Internet trolls).

When we approach it from the goal of bringing other white people with us, our focus isn't on beating them up about their white fragility, it's about helping build up their resilience to understand racism and take action for racial justice. This work is often far more emotional and spiritual than analytical, as in: "Let's look at the facts, process." We want to move white people's hearts and souls into action, which sometimes means arguing with

"We want to move white people's hearts and souls into action..."

their heads, but that is often where it stays—a head argument, rather than a heart and soul transformation. Yes, help make other white people aware of white fragility, but from the perspective of seeing how white supremacy makes white people deficient and illiterate to challenge racism. White anti-racists should want to help other white people overcome racial fragility and gain emotional health and vitality so as to meaningfully face white supremacy and join the racial justice struggle.

What I'm talking about isn't just calling in vs. calling out. It is that, but also more. It's about recognizing our work as white anti-racists as creating freedom schools for white people to get free from white supremacy. We are called to join in multiracial movements (as Black Civil Rights leaders called on whites to do in the 1960s). It's about us as white anti-racists creating opportunities for other white people to get involved in racial justice. Our work is in asking them to get involved, and supporting their growth and development to become effective racial justice activists—as opposed to letting racists on Facebook effectively distract and drain us. Our work is in encouraging them—as opposed to denouncing white people for not being on board (when the ruling class has done all they can for centuries to make white people ruthlessly and violently "oblivious"). White anti-racists must develop our capacity to bring white people in from the sidelines. Speak from your heart. Lift up the voices, experiences, and visions of Black leadership in these times, and cultivate love for other white people. We want to free as many other white people as possible from the white supremacist Voldemort which has seized their minds and souls and deformed our humanity in the service of racist evil.

Why?

Because Black Lives Matter.

Because the people of Ferguson and the Baltimore Uprisings are on the right side of history.

Let us develop white racial justice resilience for collective liberation!

To the White Anti-Racists Who Are Nervous About Stepping Up Against Racism

All over the country I'm talking with white anti-racists who are struggling with the tensions of centering Black voices and leadership and the slogan "white silence is compliance." I'm talking with experienced white anti-racists all over the country who only want to take action if a Black activist personally asks them to do it.

I'm talking with white anti-racists all over the country who both feel the enormity of this heart-breaking and powerful Black Lives Matter movement time, and are blocked from moving forward out of fear of becoming part of the problem. Here are five reflections shared with the goal of helping us step up and bring other white people with us.

1. Following Black Leadership in this time: Yes, it is essential that we are looking to Black leadership for vision, strategy, and direction. But that doesn't mean waiting for personal direction from a Black activist before taking action. It doesn't mean only going to Black-organized demonstrations and events. It doesn't mean only doing support work and staying in the background.

Black leadership for over 100 years has been calling on white people committed to racial justice to BRING racial justice leadership to white communities, to organize and mobilize white people to come together to demonstrate and protest against white supremacy and for racial justice. The time is now to organize vigils, demonstrations, speak outs, and fundraisers for BLM efforts—in white communities, white/mostly white congregations, white/mostly white networks wherever you are at.

Look for ways to build deeper, trusting relationships with Black leaders in your area, and listen for ways they are calling on white people to act, but also know that Black leaders are already spread thin organizing in their communities and building this movement. You can ask, "I'm working to get more white people involved and if you have any thoughts on how we can be most effective, let me know," and you can start getting white people on board and ready to go.

2. Take Space to Make Space: Yes, we want millions of white people to listen to and respect the voices, experiences, and leadership of Black people. And that does not mean we don't need to also bring in our voices, experiences, and leadership to help make that happen. We need to TAKE SPACE with white people and in white communities to passionately, creatively, honestly tell our stories of coming into anti-racist/racial justice consciousness as a bridge to helping other white people develop their hunger to do the same thing, and also give other white people insights and directions on how to do that.

We need to encourage, support, love on other white people who we think can move and open their hearts in this moment, and boldly ask them to join us in going to demonstrations; organizing a contingent in your congregation, neighborhood, or school to come out to protests; write letters to the editor; take public stands in support of Black-led Black Lives Matter movement.

We take space to then MAKE SPACE for white people to hear and respect Black voices, experiences, and leadership. But we can't wait for white folks to do this on their own. As white anti-racists, part of our work is taking responsibility to move other white people into action.

3. I need to be more educated/trained to take action: Yes, we need education and yes we need training. AND, we learn so much in the process of taking action,

SURJ visibility demonstration during morning commute, Walnut Creek, CA.
Photo: Felicia Gustin

joining with others, and having transformative experiences of putting our ideas into action. Many white people think they need more education and training because they are terrified of making mistakes and saying/doing the wrong things. This comes from a good place of not wanting to reinforce systems of oppression on people of color.

But here's the deal: the greatest threat to communities of color isn't the mistakes of well-intentioned white people; the greatest threat is structural and cultural anni-hilation from systems of oppression. And let me tell you: there is no such thing as "having it all figured out." We figure it out as we go. You can't workshop away your fear, but you can reach out to comrades, acknowledge what emotions are holding you back, and together support each other to step up to the historic times we live in.

We have to be careful that anti-racism for white people doesn't become a monastic life, hoping to educate one's self out of compliance with white supremacy. We aren't looking for individual enlightenment. We're looking to be part of dynamic, messy, grassroots initiatives to disrupt and challenge white supremacist capitalist patriarchy. We need to build capacity for ourselves and others to respond to calls from Black leaders on actions to take (and there are many). We need to join with national white anti-racist networks like Showing Up for Racial Justice (SURJ), AND take initiative to or-ganize events and actions in white society that ad-vance the message, vision, and demands of the Black Lives Matter movement.

> **"We need to encourage support, love on other white people who we think can move and open their hearts in this moment..."**

4. I'm afraid that everything I do will suck: On some level, nearly everything we do sucks, not just for white people, but for all of us. We must overcome the fear of how we suck, so that we can see the ways that we are also awesome, and to see the ways that we can be awesome for racial justice.

If your focus is on how whatever you do can in some way reinforce white suprem-acy, then yes, you will have a very strong sense of how everything sucks. But this is a time that calls on white people to face our demons—not through analysis alone, but through heart and soul work—and begin, in whatever ways we can, to take steps towards action for racial justice.

Meredith Martin-Moates and family with the Not My Arkansas anti-Klan, anti-racist campaign. Photo: Bryan Moates

For example, white people in Baltimore organized an action to break the curfew, with signs about racist enforcement, and about Black Lives Matter. White people in congregations around the country are organizing Black Lives Matter vigils, fundraisers for BLM, hanging BLM banners outside their churches (as many Unitarian Universalist churches are doing), and organizing rapid response groups to be able to turn people out to protests, community events, and vigils for racial justice.

In NYC Jews for Racial and Economic Justice organized civil disobedience actions with rabbis, community leaders, and activists to raise awareness in the Jewish community and unite their community with Black Lives Matter. In Knoxville, Tennessee, white racial justice activists have been part of multiracial organizing efforts resulting in Black Lives Matter demonstrations and bus rides to Ferguson. In the case of Knoxville, they have united the fight to raise the minimum wage with the fight for Black lives.

There are white anti-racists supporting the capacity of Black-led organizing by cooking meals for meetings, doing childcare, providing rides, raising money—and doing all of this with an eye towards recruiting white people who might not go to a demonstration and risk arrest, but who can and want to "throw down." And then asking white people who get involved, in whatever way, to share why they've done this with white people in their lives, to report back to their congregations or unions, share why they did it through social media, and encourage others to get involved and provide a step for how to do it.

5. But is it my place to do these things?: Yes. Do you believe in Black liberation? Do you believe in collective liberation? The changes we need will not be brought about by thousands of white people coming into anti-racist consciousness and then deciding the best thing they can do is step back. We need white anti-racists all over the country to STEP UP, but step up DIFFERENTLY than how white supremacy tells white people to do. White supremacy tells white people there is a scarcity of power and to take it for yourself. Liberation requires us to see the abundance of power and to share it. We need white anti-racists to step into liberatory power.

We need white anti-racists to be mindful of privilege, but to not forget to also be powerful for liberation. Try to cultivate a mindset that doesn't start with, "How can I not screw up?" but rather asks, "How can I be awesome for liberation?" Know that this will always include listening to others and supporting the leadership of Blacks and people of color. Also bring your own leadership, initiative, creativity, and passion to the question of, "How can we bring more and more white people into racial justice action?" This is about a future in which Black lives truly matter, and our place is in the struggle to end white supremacy and build up collective liberation.

Yes, it will be scary.

Yes, it will be awkward.

Yes, you will second guess yourself.

Yes, you will ask, "Am I really the person to be doing this?"

Tell that voice in your head to relax. Look for others to work with. Look to more-experienced white anti-racists for support. Join with people of color and Black-led efforts. Listen to the many ways white people are being asked to step up.

Take the first step.

To white people who want to see a different world where Black Lives Matter, knowing that this will also be a better world for all of us: I love you. Not because of the ways you are awesome, but also for the ways that we suck.

We can do this.

McElroy House Livingroom Conversation on Anti-Racism in Dardanelle, AR. Photo: Meredith Martin-Moates

" How can I be awesome for liberation?"

Together We Will Find the Way: An interview with DrewChristopher Joy of the Southern Maine Workers' Center

I first met DrewChristopher Joy in New Orleans after Hurricane Katrina in 2005. We were both deeply involved in the post-Katrina, Black-led reconstruction movement that was working to rebuild the majority Black working class communities destroyed by the failed government levees that flooded and destroyed large sections of the city. DrewChristopher, a white working class queer who grew up in Maine, had a tender smile when talking about working class people, and a fierce look when it came to organizing against the laws and polices that exploit and exclude working class people. After years of anti-racist organizing in Philadelphia, New Orleans, and then the San Francisco Bay Area—where he went through the Catalyst Project's Anne Braden Anti-Racist Organizing Training Program—he set his mind on returning to his home state of Maine to bring the lessons, skills, and politics he had acquired through these efforts to build up anti-racist working class power. He joined the Southern Maine Workers' Center, and quickly became a leading organizer, developing their statewide efforts.

White working class leadership and organizing is vital to ending white supremacy in this country. White working class leaders through the years—William Lloyd Garrison, Zilphia and Myles Horton, Ingrid Chapman, James Haslam, Thomas Wayne, and Rahula Janowski today—have been at the forefront of developing the politics and organizing we need to win large numbers of white people away from white supremacy and towards collective liberation. DrewChristopher and the Southern Maine Workers' Center are part of that tradition, bringing their own leadership to expand it further.

Die-In for Eric Garner Portland, ME by the Racial Justice Congress. Photo DrewChristopher Joy

Chris: How are you working to move white people into the racial justice movement in this time? What's working? And what are you learning from what works?

DrewChristopher Joy: At the Southern Maine Workers' Center, I'm working to support a majority-white working class membership to understand their relationship to a broader struggle for racial justice. My own political perspective is rooted in anti-racism and an intersectional understanding of racial, economic, and gender-based oppression; this lens consistently shapes how I think about, lead, and organize for workers' rights. For me, organizing white people into movements for racial justice is fundamentally about love for my people through both our struggles and our privileges. The SMWC strives to keep conversations about systemic racism at the forefront of our campaign work, underscoring links between the economic issues that directly impact our white working class communities and the oppressions faced by communities of color. The ultimate goal is to develop campaigns and leadership that confront the realities of class-based economic injustice while working toward the potential of a multiracial united front. Centering racial justice is integral to systemic change and collective liberation.

> **"Centering racial justice is integral to systemic change and collective liberation."**

Our work toward this vision is played out through two programming committees: Work With Dignity (WWD), currently running a campaign to raise the minimum wage in Portland and Health Care Is a Human Right (HCHR), currently involved in a statewide campaign for universal, publicly funded health care. These are base-building campaigns, which means that we are out in the streets and at community events talking to new folks about living wages and health care for all. We see these interactions as opportunities to connect people to their own experiences of injustice while pushing them on issues of racism, and we work to train up our members to engage with folks on each of these levels. At a recent HCHR member meeting, we focused on the Black Lives Matter movement and related actions that were happening in Maine. We wanted our members to feel inspired by these actions and think about how we as the HCHR campaign can respond to this political moment. We also role-played organizing conversations that regularly happen during outreach, thinking about how to address people who say things like, "I believe that healthcare is a human right, but we shouldn't pay for immigrants' health care," and, "But, don't all lives matter?"

The SMWC uses a set of human rights principles—equity, accountability, transparency, universality, participation—that we adopted from the Vermont Workers' Center

> "This approach integrates working class and poor white workers into a racial justice movement, pushing them to take action in solidarity against racism as they lead campaigns around issues that they are directly impacted by."

to guide our HCHR campaign. We've found that universality and equity in particular are great tools for pushing back against racism. I've had conversations with white people who have had a really hard time accessing healthcare who are excited about our campaign, but quickly move into scarcity thinking, worried that they might get left behind in efforts to increase access. Telling people that a central component to our campaign is universality—that everyone, without exception, by virtue of being human, is entitled to health care is a great way to shift the conversation. A follow-up question about why is that important to the campaign often ends with the individual realizing, "Right, because if we start excluding some people, then the door opens to excluding more people and then I might be left out again." We can follow this up by saying: "Under a system that is being equitably funded, in which everyone puts in what they can afford, and gets out what we need, it turns out that there really is enough for everyone. When we build a system that works for immigrants in our community, we're building a system that works for all of us." This is just an opening conversation. As we follow up with new members, we bring them into a stronger anti-racist analysis through committee work, political education trainings, and, most importantly, participation in actions and events organized by people of color-led coalitions and organizations.

This approach integrates working class and poor white workers into a racial justice movement, pushing them to take action in solidarity against racism as they lead campaigns around issues that they are directly impacted by.

Chris: How do you think about effectiveness and how do you measure it? Can you share an experience that helps you think about effective work in white communities for racial justice?

DrewChristopher: The Southern Maine Workers' Center organizing model involves making contact with hundreds of people every year and engaging with them about the economic justice issues relevant to their lives. In the past year, we've had conversations with over 900 Mainers, signed up 80 members, held two large events attended by over 70 people, and tabled or presented at over 40 events across the state. We also cosponsored five events directly related to the Black Lives Matter movement, working in solidarity with organizations such as the NAACP and Portland's Racial Justice Congress. We see the growth of our membership and the deepening of our community engagement as indicators of our increasing effectiveness. People are responding to our work and our political framework because they want to be part of an organization that is fighting for concrete victories for working class people and building up leaders for systemic change.

SMWC Heath Care as a Human Right Campaign. Photo: DrewChristopher Joy

Other measures of effectiveness can be harder to quantify and define. Our serious investments in relationships with other people and other organizations have meaningful, long-term implications, even though this work takes time and doesn't often happen on a mass scale. Similarly, when we see thousands of people on the streets it can be hard to remember that the one-on-one conversations I'm having—with strangers, with our members, and with other emerging leaders in the movement— also make a meaningful contribution. It can feel slow moving. However, I do believe that this work is contributing to the cultural and political shifts in the state being led by people of color. Ultimately, the question of effectiveness is a hard one when anti-racism is not an end goal or a campaign victory, but, rather, a practice.

Last week I spoke on a panel of activists for a multiracial audience of high school students in Portland. I was invited to speak about SMWC's work for a higher minimum wage in the city. It became clear early on in the conversation that the most pressing issue for the young people in that room was trying to make sense of the Baltimore Uprising and racism in this Black Lives Matter movement time. This event was really the heart of what I'm trying to do with my organizing: the door gets opened through the issue of raising the minimum wage, but the real opportunity is to talk about racism and racial justice.

The take-away was that many white students really want to understand enough to be in solidarity. They get their own situations—being queer and trans, being poor, watching people they love suffer. The question is how to move people from their own experiences to understanding root causes of systemic injustice. As an organizer, my job is to really show up with love and patience to those conversations while holding a strong anti-racist line and hopefully move people to action.

Chris: What are the goals and strategies (as emergent, planned, messy, and sophisticated, basic as they may be) you're operating from?

DrewChristopher: The SMWC is currently working on institutionalizing our strategies so that our political framework doesn't depend on particular organizers or members. In January, in response to the Black Lives Matter movement emerging nationally and locally, we created a document called "Together We Will Find the Way: Our Anti-Racist Organizing Commitments," which outlines a set of principles to guide our racial justice work. That statement reads:

> *We believe that it is crucial at this time to take a bold and uncompromising stance against racism. We must actively counter the politics of scarcity and fear with transformative anti-racist organizing which is the politics of abundance. As a majority white, multiracial organization, we don't claim to have all the answers, but we know that we must seek them. As this anti-racist movement continues to grow in the months and years ahead, the Southern Maine Workers' Center makes the following commitments:*
>
> *We will act in solidarity with people of color-led organizing in Maine and across the nation. We will organize around issues identified as priorities by people of color in our membership and communities. We will prioritize the leadership of people of color within our organization. We will organize white people into a movement for racial justice and collective liberation.*

This framework gives us a directive to engage with the Black Lives Matter movement. It encourages building coalitions with and directly supporting local people of color-led organizing. It centers anti-racist practices within our organization and requires us to engage in ongoing evaluation as we learn about what works and what doesn't. You can read the full text our statement here: http://www.maineworkers. org/together-we-will-find-the-way-our-anti-racist-organizing-commitments-2/.

Chris: What challenges are you facing? How are you trying to overcome them? What are you learning from these experiences?

"Organizing other white people requires both a faith in our own and each other's capacity for personal and societal transformation."

DrewChristopher: Organizing other white people requires both a faith in our own and each other's capacity for personal and societal transformation. This faith can be hard to hold onto. In organizing, we often talk about "meeting people where they are at," and while we strive to have low barriers for people to get involved, we still want to push folks to move into deeper political analysis and commitment. I've said a lot about how we think about the work and what our framework is. The challenge, of course, is in implementation. As a white person, I'm concerned with making sure that I'm meeting people where they are without letting them off the hook. How do we hold each other and ourselves lovingly accountable? How do we make sure that we are always centering an intersectional anti-oppression framework, even when speaking from our own experiences of oppression? As much as there is real potential in organizing white folks, there is also the inherent risk of de-racializing issues for the sake of unity, conflating our struggles with the struggles of people of color, or replicating racism in our own organization. I make these kinds of mistakes all the time, and when I do I try to take responsibility for them, evaluate what to do differently next time, and keep moving forward. The stakes are too high to let ourselves be held back by fears of doing it wrong.

Chris: How are you developing your own leadership and the leadership of people around you to step up in these profound, painful, and powerful Black Lives Matter movement times?

DrewChristopher: Mentorship is key to this moment. I've been fortunate to have received some really good training and political development over the years from white anti-racist and Black organizers in particular. These are the folks who urged me to move back to Maine and organize in majority white communities here. I am grateful to the people who have invested in me and loved me through my process. Mentorship is a huge gift. During the Black Lives Matter movement, I look to these mentors to help guide my work and be my political compass.

In Maine we feel the urgency of the Black Lives Matter platform in profound ways, so fostering new leadership within this movement is crucial. Our state is majority white and very working class, and we are currently seeing racism and xenophobia being used to sow fear and suspicion so that elected leaders can implement programs of austerity and state violence. These were the conditions we were working from before the Black Lives Matter movement really started to pop off, but the landscape has changed in the last five months as new organizing for racial justice has emerged in Portland and across the state, boosting existing efforts. The moment calls for us to step up our organizing work alongside the work of people of color-led organizations. We need to be helping each other get skills fast in order to respond to the moment. This means allowing new leaders to emerge more quickly than we might be used to, an adjustment for many of us who are accustomed to organizing developing at a slower pace, in which moving someone into a leadership position takes months or years. Overall, these times require flexibility in planning and letting go of some of our long-term plans in order to meet the challenges of the current moment.

Over the past few years as part of SMWC, I've done my best to pass on what I've learned to folks who are stepping up into leadership. In the past few months, I've tried to step up to support emerging leaders while also stepping back to make sure there is space for new leadership. As part of a majority white Workers' Center with a firm commitment to ending racism, I see the current moment as an opportunity to work in coalition with organizations and movements with Black leadership. I'm simultaneously continuing to push myself to better understand the conditions in Maine, implement the most effective strategies for our work, and become a better organizer in these quickly shifting conditions.

....

DrewChristopher Joy *is a white, queer, genderqueer organizer and carpenter who came up in a working class extended family that strove to uphold a commitment to racial justice in a context of struggling to make ends meet. Drew's love for white people comes from his family and the lessons they passed on. Drew is the chair of the board of directors for the Southern Maine Workers' Center (SMWC), a multiracial, mixed class membership organization that seeks to improve the lives, working conditions, and terms of employment for all Maine workers.*

To learn more about Southern Maine Workers' Center, go to www.maineworkers.org.

Racist Policing Is About Ruling Class Power, and Black Liberation Means We All Get Free

The police murder of Walter Scott in South Carolina was a tipping point in the fight against racism in policing and the criminal justice system. Two key objectives that the Black Lives Matter movement advances is to make sure we're not talking about removing racist bad apples, but changing laws, policies, and institutions that further structural racist violence, and, in thus naming the problem, move towards structural racial justice as the solution. Because many white people in the North and West want to look at the South as "really racist," we who are racialized as white need to be extra vigilant and fluent in naming and illuminating the system of white supremacy throughout the country.

"...large-scale change is both possible, and comes from everyday people building and taking power."

Secondly, we must consistently forefront the Black-led multiracial liberation movement as the center of gravity that moves our society forward. As the Black judge in South Carolina denied bail to the white police officer, I could feel W.E.B. Du Bois's essential book Black Reconstruction in my body. What's happening with the white police officer in South Carolina isn't because of how racist the South is; it's because of how vibrant, resilient, and powerful Black liberation is. Du Bois's referred to South Carolina during Reconstruction[1] as the South Carolina Commune because of the magnitude of Black and white working class leadership that took state power during that time period (with large numbers of formerly enslaved Black people governing), with the backing of white Radical Republicans (abolitionists) in Congress shaping Reconstruction and maintaining an army to help enforce it. Economic justice, public education, women's rights, and racial justice all expanded during this time period, which was then crushed by ruling class forces in the South and North, which were threatened by cross-race working class governance and power. Many say we are in a time of the "third reconstruction" (the second being the Civil Rights movement).

---

1 Reconstruction period was 1870–1877.

" ...we are standing with Black leadership for a new world."

For all of us who are white, we have a duty and an opportunity to root ourselves in the history of our people's movements, and know deeply, in our hearts and souls, that large-scale change is both possible, and comes from everyday people building and taking power. We need courageous, racialized as white, leadership to unite as many white people, organizations, congregations, schools, businesses, families, and communities as possible to the Black-led Black liberation movement, as central to an overall collective liberation agenda.

Racist policing isn't based in irrational fear, bigotry, and hate of Black people. Those are the symptoms of a much deeper fear and hatred held by ruling class power, historically and today, of Black resistance to supremacy systems, the Black radical democratic tradition, and fierce, persistent, Black leadership. For those of us who are white, it is essential to understand that we aren't just standing against Black racist victimization by the police, but we are standing with Black leadership for a new world.

SURJ Doorknocking,
Tucson, AZ.
Photo:Walt Staton

Unleashing Rage and Yearning for Liberation: The Real Lessons of Dr. King for Urban Uprisings

Let's be clear, when those in power and their media call for people to be "peaceful" in the face of endemic and sanctioned racist state violence, they aren't calling for a return to disruptive and militant nonviolent direct action unleashed by the Civil Rights movement, even if they insultingly call up Dr. King to denounce the Baltimore Uprising. These same forces decried the tactics of the Civil Rights movement as provoking violence and inviting disorder. They are part of the long, hideous campaign to gut the real lessons of the Civil Rights movement and invoke King as a way to really say: be passive, be quite, stay in your place, use the channels we designed to keep you ineffective, and by all means necessary internalize the brutality of this white supremacist capitalist system and turn it on yourself and your own community.

"For multiracial movement-building to unite people of all backgrounds for a society organized around the principle that Black lives matter."

Occupy St. Louis University, MO action.
Photo: Jenny Truax

We must not let the white supremacist power structure further rob us of the lessons of our people's movements. We must do all we can to unleash discontent, rage, pain, and yearning for liberation and stay focused on what the ruling class truly fears—poor and working class people asserting their human dignity and fighting back against a system built on extracting wealth and power from those/our communities. They use violence and devastating cultural assaults against communities of color and do everything they can to cultivate and celebrate resentment, anger, and fear in white poor and working class communities towards communities of color. For white racial justice activists, let

67

Reclaim MLK march St. Louis, MO. Photo: Janey Archey

us do all we can to aid and abet, and join with communities of color in liberation struggle, and do all we can to direct white resentment towards the powerful, while cultivating white solidarity with Black liberation and people of color-led struggles. For disruptive and militant nonviolent direct action in the spirit of the Civil Rights movement (which always focused on the systemic cause of uprisings, rather than the persecution of those initiating them). For multiracial movement building to unite people of all backgrounds for a society organized around the principle that Black lives matter. For an end to structural Black subjugation and premature death as acceptable conditions for capitalist profit and power.

Notes for a White Anti-Racist Struggling with White Friends about the Baltimore Uprising (in this case, a friend who has loved ones who are police)

I love you comrade, and I'm so grateful for the ways you throw down. What helps me in moments of frustration and disappointment while talking to white people about Black Lives Matter is to strive to balance one hard interaction with a few things that inspire me and give me positive energy to move forward. I remember white people in my life who have moved and are now working for racial justice. If it's been a particularly hard day, I watch the Helm's Deep battle in Lord of the Rings, and think, "Damn! That looked bleak. Good thing your comrades have your back."

"Keep your eyes on the prize and hearts on fire!"

For your friend, ask questions. Is this worth your time? Does this person seem movable or open? What's your relationship like and what do you want to invest? And then, what are you hoping to accomplish? Maybe moving someone from seeing the people in Baltimore as "thugs" to becoming a prison abolitionist isn't realistic. But, maybe becoming open to reading with an open mind some of the things people from the Black Lives Matter movement are writing is a good place to start.

If you do want to approach the topic, here are some thoughts. Honor what she's talking about: having friends and family in law enforcement, seeing these protests, and feeling defensive. Step into her shoes and acknowledge how it looks for her family. They may see the police as a help to their community. Just be in that. Connect to what that means to her and try to explain that all those people in Baltimore are taking to the streets for the exact same reason. They want their community to be safe. Structural poverty, the violence of the police, and racism of the criminal justice system is making their communities deeply unsafe.

I respect that she sees law enforcement that way. Ask her to consider that the people in Baltimore are giving everything they have, including risking personal safety (like her husband and friends) to bring about peace and justice. Ask her to try not to judge people, just as she doesn't want to be judged, and to ask herself, "Why are they protesting and what can I learn that can help me understand them?" Just as she wants you to understand her. Make it clear she doesn't have to agree with everything you think. However, just as she doesn't appreciate being painted a particular way, it definitely doesn't move anything forward to write off the people in Baltimore, and around the country. Those protesting that Black Lives Matter are people who are risking their lives to help make this a safer and healthier society for everyone.

Even though you may believe the criminal justice system is a racist institution, you know she and her husband want to do the right thing. I am sure we can likely all agree that major changes need to be made in this country, and that a really good place to start is actually listening to what the Black Lives Matter movement is saying.

I don't know if that resonates, but I think we need to open hearts and minds by trying to understand where white people are coming from. We need to give them space to articulate the deeper values that motivate them, and make connections between their values and the values of the Black Lives Matter movement.

Again, I think it's vital to have clear goals and expectations of what you're trying to accomplish. Far too often the biggest jackasses capture our attention, and people who are more open to movement, more open to learning and potentially acting in this moment, are ignored. I would say getting one person out to a Black Lives Matter demonstration with you, who wouldn't otherwise have come, is far more significant than twenty intense Facebook arguments.

The key, overall, is to reach white people's hearts and connect their hearts to the devastation of white supremacy in the Black community, and their (potential) desire for a world that respects everyone. Then give them things to read (a poem, a novel, or an analytical essay) coming from the Black liberation tradition or the white anti-racist tradition.

By all means, try not to let these interactions lead you to the dangerous cocktail of 30% self-righteousness and 70% hopelessness that any real change can be made. Your spirit, energy, and capacity to make an impact is precious and needed to build movement in this time. Keep your eyes on the prize and hearts on fire! Be powerful together in the streets, and we will win!

Notes to a White Anti-Racist on Struggling to Find Her Place to Speak Out, Because She Doesn't Want to Speak for People of Color

SURJ Door Knocking for BLM in Chicago, IL. Photo: Byron Durham

For me it's not about speaking for communities of color, but when it comes to racism, I'm speaking primarily for white communities. I speak out for white kids who I don't want to see grow up in this evil white supremacist system. I speak out for white people, many of us working class folk who have been screwed over generationally by the ruling classes who stoke the flames and encourage white hatred, fear, and resentment of communities of color. I speak out against ruling classes who mobilized white racism to keep both communities of color and white working class poor communities down. I speak out for white communities robbed of the humanity of people of color, while having our own humanity twisted and distorted in the service of mobilizing wealth and power to the 1%.

I bring in leadership, voices, and experiences of color, not to speak for them, but to bring lessons, vision, insight, and history from them. I present white anti-racist history and insight as well. White society needs the goal of freeing white people from the death grip of supremacy systems. Joining white people to multiracial movements for

71

collective liberation is our goal.[1] We need tens of thousands of white people courageously and passionately winning over the hearts and minds of white people, so we can all get free.

I tap into and unleash my love for people of all backgrounds and my rage for white supremacist capitalist patriarchy and support leadership of color. I also cultivate, support, encourage, and love on white anti-racist leadership to move us forward.

No, we don't want white people taking over spaces of people of color. We live in a huge country with so many people and communities. We need to remember: our primary goal isn't just speaking up in white society; it's helping break off as many white people as we can from white supremacy. Our goal is to help lead them into the long river of the multiracial democratic struggle for a better world for all of us, with racial justice at the core.

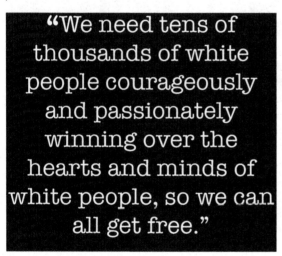

"We need tens of thousands of white people courageously and passionately winning over the hearts and minds of white people, so we can all get free."

I encourage you to breathe. Find inspiration and guidance from those whose leadership you respect. Begin finding your place. Take actionable steps into the work, for this is how you will find your place. Through the practice of applying your beliefs and breaking through fear, you will eventually find your role. Yes, it's awkward and feels confusing, because white people coming forward for racial justice, and supporting the struggles and leadership of people of color, is defying the logic and norms of white society. Going with the flow of death culture is what you're supposed to do.

Get awkward. Walk into the work, even when you're uncertain, and trust that we are making the way to freedom and structural equality, together. You are needed!

---

1   This includes all or mostly white groups/institutions/communities doing justice work with a racial justice vision/culture in alliance/solidarity with efforts from people of color.

"We're Building a Movement with the 'Young Gifted and Black Coalition' in the Lead": An Interview with Z! Haukeness on White Racial Justice Organizing in Madison, Wisconsin

For over 6 months, the Young Gifted and Black Coalition has been at the forefront of a movement on the move in Madison, Wisconsin, and Z! Haukeness, a white racial justice leader who has worked in both majority Black and majority white efforts over the past decade, has been at the heart of it. The organizing in Madison is both expansive and deep, drawing from new leadership, along with lessons and relationships forged out of past organizing, including the mass economic justice occupation of the capitol in 2011 that precipitated the Occupy Wall Street movement.

In these times of the Black Lives Matter movement, many white people are getting involved in their communities and are trying to navigate the nuances and challenges of working against white supremacist capitalist patriarchy. Z! Haukeness has been a

Allies for BLM blockade in Madison, WI. Photo: Jesse Cole

leader in white anti-racist organizing for years, and it's important for white people reading this who are newer to the work to know that Z! started off new to the work too. Z! came up through an organization called the Groundwork Collective, went through the Anne Braden Anti-Racist Organizer Training Program run by the Bay Area-based Catalyst Project, and as Z! mentions throughout the interview, their work is the result of getting involved, sticking around, learning from the people they're working with, and being part of organizations and campaigns over the long haul.

Groundwork in Madison was co-founded by white racial justice leader Laura Mc-Neill, who had been active in the global justice movement following the Seattle 1999 mass direct actions, and the post-Sept 11th anti-war movement. Laura and I were both members of the white anti-racist Bay Area-based Heads Up Collective, which formed after Sept. 11th to help unite the majority white direct action oriented anti-war movement with the people of color-led economic and racial justice movement fighting the war at home and abroad. As Laura prepared to move to Madison, Wisconsin, I remember a Heads Up meeting devoted to helping her think through starting up a similar style of group there. Z! and many other white racial justice leaders in Wisconsin came up through the group Laura helped start. I share this story to highlight the way this work is deeply relational and collective, and that experienced people's leadership in this time is needed to help create infrastructure that new people can be part of, and to encourage new people to look for opportunities to get involved in on-going local efforts, and to look for mentorship and support from those who have been around for awhile. From the outside, movements can seem mysterious and overwhelming. It is important to help demystify them and encourage people to find their path into the work.

Chris Crass: How are you working to move white people into the racial justice movement in this time? What's working? And what are you learning from what works?

Z! Haukeness: My main work to move white people into racial justice work in this time has been through working closely with a Black organization called Young Gifted and Black Coalition (YGB), which formed in response to the non-indictment of Darren Wilson and killing of Michael Brown.

My white racial justice roots are with Groundwork, a collective of white people working for racial justice that has been around for the past 10 years in Madison, Wisconsin. I have also worked closely with a few other organizations, including the No New Jail Group, a multiracial abolitionist group that formed to challenge a county-initiated proposal to build a new jail in Madison; MOSES, a predominately white faith-based organization working to oppose the jail; and the Wisconsin Network for Peace and Justice, a statewide primarily white organization working on a variety of social justice, sustainability, and peace issues around Wisconsin.

YGB is a mostly queer, female, and trans centered group dedicated to ending state violence against Black people through direct action. YGB has centered the myriad ways that state violence affects Black people, and has linked police killings with a fight to stop the building of a new jail in Dane county. State violence in Madison and Dane County is most visible through mass incarceration and vast racial disparities in the local aspects of the prison industrial complex, which are some of the worst in the country.

Young, Gifted and Black march in Madison, WI.
Photo: Nate Royko Maurer

YGB has held weekly actions since November to push for four main demands related to the jail and the mass incarceration of Black people. Both the demands and the actions have given a framework for white people to plug in and take roles to achieving a local strategy that has been largely mapped out by YGB.

There has been an incredible multiracial movement to break down jail walls and pierce liberal racism, while giving a vision of hope and possibility for true liberation. The leadership and engagement of young Black people and other people of color have been central, and the work of white people has also been key. The YGB Coalition, other people of color, and white people have all done work to educate and engage white people in the moment.

Examples of the work that white people and other allies have done to build up and support the work of YGB include showing up over and over at weekly actions—including shutting down traffic civil disobedience "die-ins," community forums, and blocking the doors of the jail for hours; hosting widely attended debates and a speaker series at the University to educate, build connections, and give credibility to YGB's work; holding a weekly series of living room conversations and fundraisers for 8 weeks at various homes to discuss YGB's work and educate white people and people of color who are not Black taking action; forming groups like Asians For Black Lives, and a budding Latin@s for Black Lives; starting a queer racial justice fund to support queer Black organizing; organizing statewide conference calls bringing together urban and rural, Black organizers and white farmers; writing statements, Op-Eds, and letters to the editor from individuals and organizations to explain racism, white privilege, and the key parts of the demands for justice locally; planning actions independently from and in accountability with YGB; organizing parent groups planning actions for children to be involved in; holding community forums to educate on the role for allies in the local movement. The list goes on and on. It is challenging to write a limited summary because the depth of work and involvement has been so vast on many fronts.

Black people, white people, and other people of color have been truly shifting the structures and systems that perpetuate state violence against Black people.

Chris: How do you think about effectiveness and how do you measure it? Can you share an experience that helps you think about effective work in white communities for racial justice?

Z!: The work of YGB has been covered by all major and alternative news sources consistently for 6 months. Everyone in Madison has heard about YGB and Black Lives Matter (BLM) and have had to decide what their position is on the killing of unarmed Black people by the police, and the gross racial disparities of policing and the prison industrial complex.

At rallies, "die-ins," public testimonies, community forums, and conference calls, we are seeing record-breaking numbers of people participating, white and people of color. More and more people are finding ways to take action, and to further commit to the struggle for Black lives and racial justice.

A concrete success came with the passage of a resolution at the County level, which hundreds of people testified on at committee meeting after committee meeting, for months. The work outlined in the resolution stops the County from building a new jail, moves towards ending solitary confinement, creates alternatives to incarceration, and seeks to end racial disparities in the criminal system. It is beautiful to see its passage as a result of a popular movement rooted in direct action, political engagement, and base building.

Many of the white people that I see showing up regularly to testify or put their bodies on the line have been involved in Groundwork in some way over the past 10 years. Either they have taken a workshop or have been more closely involved in the organization. Similarly, the base building and educational work of groups of color like Freedom Inc. have helped bring a base of leadership and analysis to the current movement moment. Multiple new organizations have grown, contributed, and strengthened over this time period as well.

Young, Gifted and Black marches in Madison, WI. Photo: Leslie Amsterdam Peterson

Personal stories of transformation are another way of measuring the effectiveness of the movement. For example, my family members are increasingly supportive. My mom talks more and more passionately about the need for change; my mom's husband, who lives in the countryside of rural Wisconsin, texted me about how much he supports the Baltimore Uprising and how the media is getting it all wrong; a friend is getting deeply engaged after being on the sidelines, unsure of how to get involved for years; and broad education is taking place in various organizations around the BLM movement, mass incarceration, and abolitionist politics.

A show of effectiveness is that this movement moment has sustained at a high level for six months and I believe deeper, thicker roots are currently forming.

Chris: What are the goals and strategies (as emergent, planned, messy, and sophisticated, basic as they may be) you're operating from?

Z!: My goals for engaging white people who are waking up to racism and police violence, or getting more deeply committed to racial justice, are to help move them, in whatever way they can, to participate towards achieving Black liberation, Black power, Black queer power, Black trans power, Black migrant power, Black disability power, Black cis-women's power, Black cis-men's power; and to end violence against Black people. Both YGB and BLM have an incredible intersectional analysis to help guide this work forward.

YGB Demands

As stated above, YGB's vision has been the guiding light for this movement moment locally. This includes their demands, but also their approach of direct confrontation of power structures, and pushing people to a new understanding of white supremacy and the immediate need for change.

The demands around the jail are: (1) no new jail or major renovations to the current jail, (2) release 350 Black people incarcerated due to racial and economic oppression, (3) end solitary confinement, and (4) divert money that would be spent on incarceration to Black-led alternatives and community-based solutions to addressing racial disparities.

Since Tony Robinson was killed and the police officer who killed him was not charged, making National headlines, the group has added two demands: (1) the United Nations must do a truly independent investigation into the murder of Tony Robinson and the gross racial disparities of Dane County, and (2) there must be true community control over the police to make decisions on policies, practices, procedures, hiring, and firing.

Black Lives Matter (BLM) Framework

YGB, myself, and others have also followed the BLM framework and worked to honor the leadership and history of the movement. We were able to bring Opal Tometi, one of the co-founders of BLM, to Madison to speak to a few hundred people about the movement and keep the BLM framework central to our local work. We have always told the story of Alicia Garza creating the hashtag and partnering with Patrisse Cullors and Opal to create the organization, highlighting the importance that this was created by two queer women and the daughter of Nigerian immigrants. We have worked hard and learned from their framing that centers state violence against all Black lives, particularly highlighting those whose deaths are often forgotten, such as Black cisgender and trans women.

White Anti-Racist Basics

I have also been operating under principles that I have learned over the years through white racial justice organizing and from mentors and educators. Some of the principals include: Show up, listen, support, engage in activity rather than critiquing from the sidelines, get out front and be loud for racial justice when the time is right, stay in the background when the time is right, educate other white people about racism so it doesn't all fall on people of color, do personal education and skill-building, engage more white people in action, find ways for white people to bring their full leadership to the fore in respectful ways, and recruit resources—including financial support to the movement.

Building an Anti-Racist White Majority

There is great potential right now to move white people to consciousness around white supremacy. We have a chance to really shift the scales and create long-lasting structure and momentum to continue engaging large numbers of white people to work for racial justice in an accountable way. We still have a long way to go, but we are making moves.

Chris: What challenges are you facing? How are you trying to overcome them? What are you learning from these experiences?

Z!: Over the years I have often walked the line of working with predominantly people of color organizations while also working in predominately white organizations with a focus on racial justice. Most of my work in this moment has been working closely with people of color, while much of my role has been to engage white people and move a strategy forward in a predominately white community with white power holders.

While this isn't a universal role for white people to play, it has been a natural role for me due to years of personal and organizational relationship building. My relationships with others in YGB have come largely from my relationships with Groundwork, Freedom Inc., Operation Welcome Home, and other local groups as well as personal relationships. For many years I have learned from mentors, shown up, made mistakes, built relationships, struggled through relationships, taken action, made great strides, fallen down with shame and grief and confusion, and gotten back up to repeat the cycle. I have done this in community and the importance of organization shines through in this process.

While the work of maintaining multiracial connections and relationships in organizing is crucial work, it is important that white people work with other white people and sometimes that means having little direct contact with people of color in leadership.

Also in this time of an amazing flow of energy, a window has opened in this movement moment, which also calls on a huge flow of time and energy put in by organizers. Myself and others have put in hours and hours of volunteer time and have had trouble balancing this work responsibility with our other work and life responsibilities. For many years of doing work as an "ally" I have pushed myself to work, and work until exhaustion and burnout. I felt I was only doing enough for racial justice if I physically and emotionally couldn't get out of bed because I was too worn out. Then

I was doing enough. I have moved along that path to now see my own health and well being as necessary to my effectiveness in being a leader for racial justice. I am working to practice and cultivate resiliency, and while there are still ups and downs, and periods of burnout due to the high intensity of the work, I have found better balance and have limited the depth of the low points.

> **"Black people, white people, and other people of color have been truly shifting the structures and systems that perpetuate state violence against Black people."**

Another challenge I have been facing is related to "calling white people in" rather than calling them "out," while showing anger and rage for the system that many white people in power are upholding. Groups similar to Groundwork across the country often use the principle of calling white people in and building with love; however, it has been important to directly challenge the racism of the police chief and others in power. While these politicians and public officials may be well-intentioned, as representatives and enforcers of systems that are inflicting state violence and killing Black people, they need to be challenged publicly.

Similarly, I have struggled with the fine line of calling white people in, while directly challenging those who say they are for justice but consider YGB too radical or "violent." The Midwestern and liberal niceties, and a broad thinking that Madison is progressive, have gotten us to where we are with drastic racial disparities. It has been a lesson that "calling in" isn't always nice or without conflict, and has pushed my own aversion to direct conflict. Having white people show anger and frustration, as well as love and compassion, while participating in controversial actions and really being challenged to get uncomfortable and understand the need for more direct tactics and conversations have helped to dissipate this dilemma.

We need both. We need to directly challenge those who are upholding the system, and create spaces and opportunities to bring in those willing to get educated to fight against it.

Chris: How are you developing your own leadership and the leadership of people around you to step up in these profound, painful, and powerful Black Lives Matter movement times?

> **"...we are building a movement, we are making waves, working hard to plant roots and growing beautiful change."**

Z!: The energy, momentum, and community that has been built and strengthened over the past 6 months thrives on natural and organized opportunities for leadership development.

The community forums, teach-ins on legislation, debates between YGB and the Sheriff, nationally recognized speakers, core group and base education, one-on-ones, and door knocking are all ways that YGB, Groundwork, and various organizations have been engaging in leadership development and political education. However, possibly the most powerful has been the shared work together—when we spend long hours in strategy meetings in various organizations, when we greet one another at events, when we strategize over dinner, when we laugh and joke over drinks, when we check in at rallies and actions, when we wait through long hours of testimony or deliberation at County Board committee meetings, and when we have long one-on-one conversations about how we are struggling personally or organizationally and how to move through it together.

We are loving each other and growing with each other. We are having conflict with each other and challenging each other to grow. We are teaching one another and getting on each other's nerves. We are doing our own work and we are bringing in new people; we are building a movement; we are making waves, working hard to plant roots, and growing beautiful change.

I'm always learning by doing; learning by reflecting; learning by listening to those around me, reading books, and watching YouTube videos. I'm learning by making mistakes, by having some new triumphs, by pushing myself, hard, and by being gentle with myself. I'm reaching out to community and I'm taking care of those I love around me who are giving so much.

We have been developing new leadership by creating avenues for people to get engaged, to learn, to take action, to love, to hurt, and to fan the flames of change; to be part of the life-or-death movement to make Black Lives Matter.

....

Z! Haukeness *is a community organizer in Madison, Wisconsin, working on various racial and social justice issues locally and nationally. Z! is trans and gender nonconforming and carries the privilege and oppression of this identity in his work for liberation. Thanks to Sara McKinnon, Karma Chávez, and Laura McNeil for their help editing.*

To learn more about the Young Gifted and Black Coalition, go to www.ygbcoalition.org.

Victories Belong to the People: On May Day and Everyday

The charges of homicide against the 6 police offices in Baltimore isn't "the system working"; it's the power of militant and disruptive people's movements breaking the rules designed to keep us ineffective, and changing what's politically possible. No Baltimore Uprising, no charges. The people's uprising in Ferguson. and the powerful mass disobedient actions around the country have been changing the political landscape and reigniting Black liberation vision, demands, culture, audacity, and hope around the country, united for a world in which Black Lives Matter.

With the charges in Baltimore coming on May Day, International Workers Day, it's important to reflect on where change comes from and to remember that victories towards justice belong to the people. May Day comes out of the 1886 anarchist/socialist-led labor movement's fight for the 8-hour work day. The state of Illinois executed five anarchist labor leaders/activists in Chicago, after a police-instigated riot with mostly working class European Americans; this was before many of them became racialized as white and granted access to white entitlement and privilege as a way to divest them of working class solidarity and disobedience to the ruling order. People who fought the rule of the bosses and the state, people like Lucy and Albert Parsons, August Spies, and Lizzie Holmes, and millions of working class people who have come together to fight back are the reason we have every pro-worker victory.

> **"Whenever small and large changes are made, let us connect to the powerful legacies of our ancestors who fought for a better world."**

The ruling order thrives on us feeling powerless, internalizing their logic that all the positive changes have been the result of the system correcting itself, or the benevolence/philanthropy of the ruling class. Whenever small and large changes are made, let us connect to the powerful legacies of our ancestors who fought for a better world. Our ancestors who fought for future generations. And let us recognize that we are those future generations they fought for. Let us continue to change what is politically possible through militant, disobedient, visionary people's movements rooted in love and rage.

Rising Up to the Challenges of Our Time: An Interview with Zoë Williams on White Racial Justice Organizing in Denver, Colorado

From Charleston to McKinney to Baltimore to Ferguson, the epidemic of anti-black racist violence is screaming all around us, and white people in the millions are being pulled out of the indifference coupled with moral superiority built on empty platitudes of "being good white people" and are taking the red pill to wake up to the reality of institutional white supremacy.

In these Black Lives Matter movement on the move times there is a deep need for white people coming into consciousness about racism to have positive white anti-racist examples and role models to help them navigate the difficulty of taking effective action for racial justice, and developing a healthy self-identity rooted in collective liberation, rather than supremacy systems.

This interview is with Denver-based white racial justice leader, Zoë Williams. From building campaigns for transit justice in multiracial working class communities to leading accessible and engaging political education about racial justice with white working class communities, Zoë Williams is a younger generation, white, working class, queer, genderqueer leader and parent in the Denver Metro Area, whose approach to organizing and movement building is rooted in love for the people and their belief in grassroots power to win structural change.

I first meet Zoë in 2001, when they reached out for support dealing with sexism in their activist community as a fifteen-year-old femme queer who was fired up, but was getting shut out, rather then lifted up. I knew then that Zoë was the kind of leader we needed to build effective and transformational movements, and I'm deeply grateful for this opportunity to lift up their leadership to help guide thousands of white people coming into consciousness and looking to step up in these Black Lives Matter times.

Chris Crass: How are you working to move white people into the racial justice movement in this time? What's working? And what are you learning from what works?

Zoë Williams: My orientation in my community is to wear a lot of different hats. I work as a transit organizer for 9to5 Colorado, a women's economic justice organization, building campaigns around transit justice and gentrification. In the Denver Metro Area we are seeing a lot of intense structural violence with communities facing transit fare hikes, cuts in bus service, rising rent costs, low wages, and high cost of living. We look to women who are people of color, immigrants, currently or formerly homeless, fleeing violence, and working low-wage jobs as leaders who define our issues and create our vision for change.

I am also a street medic trainer, first aid instructor, community health advocate, and folk medicine maker. Street medicine is where I learned many of my lessons in taking action against racism. My mentors in street medicine were elders in the community with experience going back to the Civil Rights movement and Wounded Knee. It gave me a tangible space to practice solidarity alongside the American Indian Movement, immigrant rights struggle, and other local work. I don't run as a street medic often anymore, but I offer trainings so that more folks can have access to that opportunity.

Zoë Williams speaking at Transit Justice Rally in Denver, CO. Photo: Alex Landau

Recently, healing justice activists like Leah Lakshmi Piepzna-Samarasinha have created a really powerful model to mobilize healers, make care accessible, and support movements through health work. After participating in the 2014 Healing Justice for Black Lives Matter action, I've been exploring new tactics in redistributing healthcare, knowledge, and resources while supporting self-care in my community.

One of my greatest passions is political education, and I have been providing trainings to groups ranging from middle school students and food justice activists to healthcare workers about white supremacy, solidarity, and allyship. The goal of these trainings is to get more language and analysis out to white people who may or may not view themselves as "activists" with a push toward action. I want to get as many people the skills or words they feel they need to enter into conversations about racism and bring their networks into anti-racist action as possible.

Over the past few months I have been working with a group that just formed as a SURJ (Showing Up for Racial Justice) Denver chapter. We've been really focused on sharing principles, building process, and creating relationships in our community. Now we are ready for action!

Finally, and on a much smaller, more personal scale, I am a parent. My partner and I have dedicated our library to lifting up the stories and voices of people of color so that our children grow up with the language, tools, and stories to build their understanding of race. Another part of parenting is building relationships with other families and finding ways to bring racial justice into those spaces. Having lived and organized in the same space for most of my life, I really appreciate having a lot of different avenues and scales for action.

> **"Lead with your hearts. It is the part of you that is most free from the stains of white violence."**

Chris: How do you think about effectiveness and how do you measure it? Can you share an experience that helps you think about effective work in white communities for racial justice?

Zoë: Efficacy is a tricky and subjective thing, particularly considering the communities my work spans. To me, it boils down to two things: movement and context. When we get people and power to move from the status quo towards a vision of a liberated future, we have been effective.

Sometimes that movement is small in the grand scheme of things. One example came from a friend attending a rally against police violence this spring. This person made a sign that said something along the lines of "End White Supremacy." As a white person that was raised in a household and community where overtly racist language and ideology was the norm, this person had never taken a visible stance in this way to publicly oppose white supremacy. However, after being inspired by the Black Lives Matter movement and some organizing training, they took this step. That is worth celebrating.

On a larger scale, I look to some of the campaigns I have been able to work on with 9to5. As a grassroots organization, our leaders determine our issues, campaigns, and priorities. So far, I have worked on campaigns to bring bus routes back into service, fight fare hikes, and fight gentrification. Through our organization, we have been able to bring allies from larger organizations, faith communities, and labor to join in support and solidarity. I feel proud to see white people looking at their resources critically and dedicating them toward the issues that communities of color, women, queer people, people with disabilities, people navigating homelessness, and poor and working class people define as important.

Chris: What are the goals and strategies (as emergent, planned, messy, and sophisticated (basic as they may be) you're operating from?

Zoë: One of the most important aspects of being a white person involved in anti-racist organizing is having accountable and lasting relationships. We need to be involved in accountable and lasting relationships with leaders, organizations, and communities of color. The way that white supremacy rears its head in the Denver area is going to look very different than Ferguson, Baltimore, or some of the other cities that have captivated the nation. When the stakes feel so high, it is easy to rush past the relationship step and try to take action. Our connections help me and my communities know when to show up to the work in ways that support local movements in a meaningful way. Also, as white people we need to be building long-term relationships with other white people so that we can support one another's growth.

A call from many leaders of color in the Denver Metro Area is for white people to participate in the redistribution of resources, so this has felt like a very important strategy to commit to. Money and resources have a deep connection with white supremacy. The poor and working class white communities I am from and live and typically work in have complicated relationships with money and resources. Answering this call has meant more than passing a hat or giving to a fundraiser. It has involved collective consciousness work around white supremacy, classism, and solidarity work.

With regard to some of the interpersonal and family based work I do, one of the biggest goals is to create dialogue and a feeling that we can do something. So many white parents are horrified that their kids could end up being Darren Wilson or the police officer that attacked the youth in McKinney. However, they are scrambling to find tools to have honest conversations about white supremacy at home or on the playground. Incidentally, those are some of the most powerful spaces to reach young people to take action against white supremacy.

After all, the spread of the information about the racist brutality at the pool in McKinney is due in part to video and witness statements of white teenagers who saw the police attacking and knew it was racially motivated. Fifteen-year-old Brandon Brooks took the now infamous video and told the media about his experience watching the police target youth of color while he continued to film the incident and stated, "They're just going to discriminate against them because they're black." Other young white people lifted up the experiences of the young women of color and affirmed that the incident began when white adults began verbally abusing youth of color. These youth leveraged their privilege in brave ways to ensure that a white supremacist narrative did not prevail.

Our task is to raise more children to do that, and my goal is to make it easier through discussion groups, book lists, gatherings, and one-on-one support with the parents in my life to keep going to the hard conversations.

Chris: What challenges are you facing? How are you trying to overcome them? What are you learning from these experiences?

Zoë: In the wake of the horrific racist terrorist attack on Emanuel AME Church, there are a lot of white folks who want to do something, but they are afraid. The stakes feel really high, the reality is so painful, and people are going against a lifetime of teaching. It is important to create a space that is not taking resources or energy from efforts led by communities of color that allows white folks to learn to move through fear. Sometimes all this takes is reminding people, "Yes, we are all going to make mis-

Denver, CO Pride Anti-Police Brutality Contingent. Photo: Direct Autonomous Media

takes in this work, and that will be okay. We will also make amends. The risks of doing nothing far outweigh the risks of doing something imperfectly." Other times it is reminding people what skills and talents they bring to the work so that they can see themselves as strengths and assets.

After the attacks in Charleston, I was asking a friend what his faith community needed for support from allies. He told me, "We need less analysis and more action from our allies. Lead with your hearts. It is the part of you that is most free from the stains of white violence." Particularly in our new SURJ chapter, this is one of our greatest goals at the moment. We are working together to get one another out of the analytical thinking space and into heart-centered action.

Part of the challenge is that a lot of work around white supremacy and white anti-racism is housed in academia. Most people around me were exposed to the concepts of white supremacy and white privilege in college. The language, theory, and process of academic-based anti-racism is very inaccessible and difficult to put into practice. After all, if you've spent two-to-six years writing papers about all of the bad things white people do, it is hard to come out the other side as a white person ready for action. Even more problematic is that many people don't have access to higher education. Growing up in a working class town, most of my friends did not get to attend education outside of high school, and those who did couldn't start until adulthood. That's only thinking about class barriers to higher ed. Political education is incredibly valuable, but we need to move conversations from the "Ivory Tower" back into the hands of our communities.

Popular education is one of my favorite tools to create shared and evolving consciousness about race, white supremacy, and intersections with other identities. Popular education workshops begin with the belief that people already know about these issues, they just need tools to break them down and take action. One of my favorite tools that has been passed down to me by many teachers is using a timeline of historic events, usually centered around an issue. When 9to5 first started pushing for affordable transit, many of our members and constituents felt that there was no hope in winning a campaign on the issue. We created a timeline with transit justice events starting with Rosa Parks that covered Civil Rights era actions, ADAPT and the disability rights movement that was so powerful in Colorado, and more recent organizing like the LA Bus Riders Union. People explored the timeline and put notes about what they were doing, or how they felt about different events. The first time I did the activity in a meeting, the notes were amazing. People wrote things like, "We are finishing our elder's work," and, "I want to do something like this for my family."

> "Political education is incredibly valuable, but we need to move conversations from the "Ivory Tower" back into the hands of our communities."

Even when we have hit hard times, going back to that timeline has helped people power through the campaign. Recently the Regional Transportation District Board of Directors approved a fare hike, and our members said, "We just have to fight harder. This is not over. We won when we took over their meeting, and we will win again."

Chris: How are you developing your own leadership and the leadership of people around you to step up in these profound, painful, and powerful Black Lives Matter movement times?

Zoë: One of the amazing lessons that I have learned from the Black Lives Matter movement is the absolute vital importance of developing leadership from youth, poor, working class, female, gender nonconforming, femme, transgender, and queer people. This translates so clearly to white anti-racist work, and has become the crux of my own goals in finding leaders around me.

"Because of the ways patriarchy, classism, heterosexism, transphobia, and other painful systems have impacted our lives, it can be hard to feel capable of leadership."

As a queer femme young person, I needed a lot of pushing to believe I could do the work that I ended up doing. My mentor once joked that he had to put four times the work into building my confidence than a middle class straight man would have required, and that was just to get me to speak my opinion in a meeting. It's important for me to remember that now when urging people to start hard conversations, or be willing to answer the call to take risks at actions. Because of the ways patriarchy, classism, heterosexism, transphobia, and other painful systems have impacted our lives, it can be hard to feel capable of leadership. That said, those experiences are all the more reason leaders with those experiences need to be invested in and given the resources to take powerful actions for change.

....

Zoë Williams *is a queer and genderqueer parent, witch, community organizer, popular education facilitator, gardener, herbalist, and lover of cats. They have been organizing in the Denver Metro Area for over 15 years with a broad range of issues, campaigns, and coalitions.*

Every White Person Is Aiding and Abetting Terrorism Unless Naming Institutional and Cultural White Supremacy in the Charleston Massacre

Every white person who refers to Charleston as "incomprehensible racial tension" (which narrates it as equal people who equally don't like each other, and it's impossible to understand) is providing cover to murderous, historically rooted, structural, and cultural white supremacy that is growing stronger every day.

Protesting a Pro-Confederate Flag Rally in Richmond, Virginia.
Photo: Leah Hunt-Hendrix

Every white person who refers to the shooter as a "disturbed individual full of hate" without talking about the pathological culture of white supremacy that filled him with hate and gave him a target for his rage, is furthering the pathological culture that is simultaneously horrified by these acts, and refuses to acknowledge what they reveal about our society.

Every white person who calls the shooter insane is by default normalizing and perpetuating structural and individual white supremacist violence. Every white person who says this is a human tragedy, not about race, is saying that Black life on its own isn't worthy of national tragedy, and must be made raceless—removed from history, context, and meaning.

91

Because, once we put in into historical context, this isn't just a national tragedy by an individual madman. It is the latest assault in a long and devastating tradition of anti-Black racism perpetuated by white people who feel, first, entitled to blame Black people and people of color for all the rage, anguish, and pain they experience, and, second, that they are entitled to enact horrific violence—from lynching, to burning down Black neighborhoods, to calling the police on a Black teenagers' pool party, to shooting over and over again into a car full of Black kids because you thought their music was too loud, to walking into a prayer circle at a leading Black church and relentlessly murdering the Black people praying because "the Blacks are coming for our white women."

Every white person focused on explaining how much they personally like Black people and so therefore racism can't exist needs to take a long hard look at how the shooter clearly had a plan, was methodical, and patiently implemented horrific acts, while ensuring survivors could spread the news of this terrorist attack, to further terrorize the Black community.

BLM rally at MN State Fair. Photo Erika Sanders

White people need to sit silently and ask, "What is the message the shooter wanted communicated? How is that message institutionally and culturally represented and expressed all around us?" And then respond: "If we truly abhor this devastating act, then we must recognize it as terrorism and seek to understand the worldview, the institutional backing, and political agenda this terrorism is imbedded in."

We must recognize that white indifference and denial is key to giving space for this terrorism to operate and thrive, and commit ourselves to destroying the vast networks of support giving rise to this terrorist attack against Black members of a Black church, rooted in Black liberation struggle and a vision of beloved community for all.

White people, our work is to turn the horror and heartbreak we are feeling, and do everything we can to move white people in the millions into active racial justice efforts for Black Lives Matter and multiracial democracy springing from structural and cultural change. And for all of us who are white anti-racists, our job is to help free our white people's minds from the ways white supremacy trains us to understand the world.

Most white people don't wake up and say, "I want to support white supremacy today," but they stand up on the unconscious conveyor belt moving them forward along the normalized white supremacist path. As Kentucky-based white anti-racist leader Sonja de Vries reminds us, we must work to support other white people to join us on this journey, rather than push them away for not already being with us or using the wrong words.

We must free ourselves and other white people from the murderous logic that allows these acts of terrorism to continue, looking for the openings with other white people to go deeper, rather than only seeing the closings. The future of our society is at stake, the health of our hearts and souls are at stake, the possibility of our children being the next shooter or the next freedom rider is at stake. I know it is heartbreaking looking deep into the face of this tragedy. But the more you look, the more you will realize that your heart is breaking free from white supremacy and opening to the possibility of ending this death culture and achieving collective liberation.

Notes for White Religious Leaders Who Want to Turn White Faith Communities into Spiritual Strongholds for Racial Justice

Around the country, white people are searching for direction in the midst of heartbreak and outrage as anti-Black racism murders young Black people in the streets at the hands of police, murders Black people praying in their historic church in Charleston, and burns churches and distributes hate literature around the country.

White faith leaders across denominations and faiths are struggling to meet their white faith communities where they're at and move them towards racial justice in these Black Lives Matter movement times. In responding to questions from a young adult Unitarian Universalist religious leader, I made these notes to support her and other white faith leaders to step up and lead white people away from the ruling class worldview of white supremacy and towards beloved community and collective liberation.

....

Dr. Cornel West and Rev. Jim Wallis march in Ferguson, MO.
Photo: Margaret Ernst

1. We must nurture the hearts and souls of our faith communities to be able to look at the racist institutional and cultural violence that is burning all around us. To acknowledge the despair, the pain, the heartbreak, and to collectively grieve—to assume that everyone there, on some level, is grieving and to invite them into that space, rather than assume they are indifferent and uncaring, even if one could assume that

about them from their actions/inaction. We are not here to pass judgment on who we think they are, but to create support for the people they want to be, who we know they can be, who these times call on our people to be.

2. We must root ourselves in our spiritual super powers through prayer, song, meditation, or whatever else will help, to ground people in the power of our faith, in the power of the divine, in the power of all that is sacred, to then call forward our outrage for the racist assaults on Black humanity.

3. We must connect to and express our outrage for the monstrosity of racism in every individual act, institutional policy, and piece of government legislation that forces us to affirm that "Black Lives Matter." Our outrage that the churches of the Black community are on fire, that Black church members are forced to go armed to the pews and pray for their safety and the safety of their loved ones each time they go to church,

> **"I believe in our ability to do this."**

to a pool party, to the corner store, to life in America. Our outrage that so many white faith communities are failing to even recognize, let alone wage all-out heart and soul-saving campaigns against the evil of racism that creates spiritual and emotional poverty in white communities.

4. The spiritual and emotional poverty that raised the twenty-one-year-old young person who became a white supremacist mass murderer in Charleston exists because so many of the white leaders and institutions of our society have turned their hearts and heads away from the epidemic of racism, and have chosen the path of self-congratulatory post-racial or colorblind indifference, or have abandoned the public words of racism while maintaining active support for the public manifestations and expressions of institutional and cultural racism.

5. All of us who are white have a responsibility to raise white children to know the full expression of racism in society, as well as anti-racist commitment, values, and action. We must play an active role in helping end the spiritual and emotional poverty of white supremacy that trains white people to inhabit resentment, isolation, depression, self-pity, and self-hatred and direct all of it towards communities of color, with anti-black racism at the heart of this devastation.

6. The truth of the matter is this—yes, we must do all we can to stop the burning of Black churches and to support the rebuilding of those that racists and racism have burned down. But we must go deeper, and, for this, we must pray; we must call upon the most meaningful and soul-nourishing attributes of our religions, of our faiths, because the truth is, white supremacy has long been burning down the heart, soul, and values of white faith communities, even if our buildings stand sturdy. As white people, in a white supremacist society, we are either actively anti-racist, or we are complicit in the violent, nuanced, everyday mechanisms of racism. As white people, we are either actively cultivating anti-racist liberation knowledge, practice, and culture or we are living, day in and day out, in the foul spiritual and cultural poverty of white supremacy.

The fate of our collective souls is at stake in the struggle against racism and for racial justice. And we must call out to rebuild white faith communities, to rebuild our faiths, to fight for the souls of white people from racism.

7. I believe in our ability to do this. And, here, I highly encourage sharing stories of your faith community, your denomination, or tradition—as well as yourself—confronting the horrors of racism and choosing racial justice. Share stories of the fear, the confusion, the cluelessness, and the heartbreak—but also of the courage, the relationships made in the work, finding your way, and becoming effective. And, as much as possible, share stories of groups of white people, white people of your faith or others, acting in collective ways to join with Black liberation movement historically and the Black Lives Matter movement today. Stories of white people showing up and stepping up for racial justice. Stories of seeing yourself and/or other white people wrestling with white supremacy in their hearts and minds—and, through taking action in the world, expanding love in their lives, while standing on the side of love in the world. Share stories of coming into consciousness and into life-affirming, dynamic cultures of liberation.

8. And while we are putting forward a vision of white faith communities as white racial justice faith communities, let's put forward the need to both join in multiracial racial justice movements, and look for ways to join with, and support, Black-led efforts in these times. AND to develop real efforts to take on and end the spiritual and emotional poverty in white communities—through learning about the people's history of the United States and around the world, to develop anti-racist liberation literacy. For us to learn about the movement for Black Lives Matter in these times, and how a world that truly values all Black humanity would be a fundamentally better world for all of us. For us to learn about white anti-racists throughout history who

white people can feel proud of and who they can look to as role models of another way, and for people of color to know that there have always been white people who choose another path.

9. To help prepare for your sermon or worship service, my advice is this. As spiritual/religious white anti-racist leaders, yes we must raise critiques of existing racist society, but we should have a realistic sense of where the people of our faith communities are at, particularly the white ones, and we must be careful not to take our anger, sadness, and despair about white supremacy out on the white people of our faith community.

"Share stories of coming into consciousness and into life-affirming, dynamic cultures of liberation."

They too have been raised in the spiritual and emotional poverty of white supremacy; our task is to help them recognize the racist conditions in ways that galvanize them to change them, and give them tools and advice, through stories from your own and other's personal journeys, to help them work through denial, guilt, self-hate, and fear. We are not here to rage at white people for their lack of anti-racist involvement, though there may be times when that is called for; we are spiritual leaders who want to love the wickedness of white supremacy out of them and the white community. Our goal isn't to prove to others that we aren't racist; it is to develop the capacity of our faith community, and other white people, to rise up against white supremacy.

We must not hate our people for where they are, but see where they—or a good number of them, enough to build momentum and leadership to move our communities into action—can go. We must help connect anti-racist work to the truth of their faith values, and to the aspirations of the people they yearn to be.

10. This is divine work. Ground yourself, wail and pray to and with the movement ancestors that nourish you, hold on to the ones you love, and stand before and with your faith community and unleash the passion, the courage, the outrage,

the hope, and the truth of your soul, with the goal of leading your/our people towards beloved community, towards the multiracial racial justice movement, towards the living expression of your faith's deepest values and commitments.

Help our people see, in your courage, in your truth telling, in your pain and vulnerability, that they too can be courageous—amidst their brokenness, their imperfections, their grief, their uncertainty—and they too can step up for racial justice in these times. Help our people see that Black Lives Matter is a vision and movement in which we can all get free from the poverties of white supremacy and end the anti-Black racist violence tearing apart our country.

> "Help our people see,
> in your courage,
> in your truth telling,
> in your pain and
> vulnerability, that
> they too can
> be courageous..."

Answering the Call: White People Showing Up for Racial Justice: An Interview with Carla Wallace, Dara Silverman and Sam Hamlin of the Showing Up for Racial Justice Network

For the past seven years, white anti-racists from around the country—from Highlander Center in Tennessee, to the Coalition of Anti-Racist Whites in Washington, to Groundwork Collective in Wisconsin, to Fairness Campaign in Kentucky, to Catalyst Project in California—have been building up a national network to engage and move white people towards racial justice action. Rooted in longstanding white anti-racist efforts and leadership, along with strong relationships with organizers and leaders of color, Showing Up for Racial Justice (SURJ) has been building infrastructure, relationships, shared values, and membership to respond to the call from Black leaders and leaders of color to move white people into action. From the Arizona anti-immigration struggle in 2010 to the murder of Trayvon Martin, SURJ has been bringing national leadership to help give focus, energy, and effective leadership to white anti-racist efforts. Since Ferguson, SURJ has literally been surging with new members, new chapters, and a growing role of convening national calls to help inform, equip, and mobilize a massively expanding base of white people into racial justice action.

This interview with national leaders of SURJ—Sam Hamlin, Dara Silverman, and Carla Wallace—draws out lessons from their work to help all of us who want to move more white people into effective and accountable racial justice action.

SURJ Members Preparing For BLM Door Knocking San Francisco, CA.
Photo Felicia Gustin

Chris Crass: How are you working to move white people into the racial justice movement in this time? What's working? And what are you learning from what works?

Sam Hamlin: Our current focus is on strengthening white anti-racist leadership locally and nationally with Showing Up for Racial Justice (SURJ). SURJ is a national network of affiliated groups committed to organizing white people for racial justice. SURJ is putting energy into building up infrastructure to support leadership development and capacity building on the local and regional level. We do this through recruitment, leadership development, mentorship, and providing people with multiple meaningful and accessible entry points, and action steps in solidarity with the movement for black lives. We encourage an approach that centers peer support and skill-sharing. We're now working with seventy-five groups and affiliates across the country and thousands of individuals.

"We want to reach white people who are already in action for social justice, and white people who care, and get them to show up in action for racial justice..."

We are in a moment in history when the violence of police brutality against communities of color as well as powerful Black-led struggles for justice are in the national spotlight. For the first time in many years, millions of white people in the U.S. are being forced to confront the issue of racism and, inevitably, to make a choice of which side of history we are on: are we going to align with institutions of white supremacy that justify the murder of people of color at the hands of police? Or are we going to be on the side of the powerful Black-led resistance and the movement for collective freedom and justice? It is times like these that hold the potential for shifts of consciousness on society-wide levels. We are seeing that with the thousands of white people who are wanting to take action in solidarity with the Movement for Black Lives.

What has really struck me about organizing in this time is how many white people are wanting to do something, and how absolutely necessary it is for folks to have meaningful ways to move into action, and ways to sustain that movement for the long haul. We have been addressing this need by providing clear action steps that can be taken up and adapted for local contexts; reducing isolation by creating spaces where local leaders can share successes, challenges, and questions; and building leadership through trainings, mentorship, and moving deeper into the work together nationally.

Carla Wallace: Ever since we began SURJ in the midst of the racial backlash to the election of the nation's first Black president, the work has been driven by the urgency to grow the numbers of white people challenging racism and creating a visible, different way to be white for other white people to gravitate to. Our sisters and brothers of color asked this of us in 2009 and have been asking this since the 1960s. SURJ was founded after Barack Obama was elected, when there was a marked rise in right-wing militias and increased attacks on people of color. Leaders of color came to the founders of SURJ and said we need there to be more white people speaking up and taking action against this, not just people of color. While there have always been white people who have broken with white supremacy and supported racial justice in this country's history, we have been unable to organize the numbers needed, when joined with people of color, to break the divide by which those in power maintain oppressive control.

With so many white people trying to find their way into effective, meaningful work for racial justice, we feel a great responsibility in SURJ to help that happen. SURJ supports local people already engaged in racial justice to organize other white people into visible, effective action in accountable relationship to people of color-led efforts. We want to reach white people who are already in action for social justice, and white people who care, and get them to show up in action for racial justice and to grow the regional and national connections among white people doing this work.

What seems to be working is supporting people on the ground, doing this work (or wanting to) around the country. With the need for SURJ support exploding in the wake of the killings of Black young people by police, including Trayvon Martin and Michael Brown, and queer Latina Jessie Hernandez, and so many others, initiating contact with and responding to the need for organizing support has stretched the SURJ capacity to the limit. So, supporting people to grow relationships with one another, and setting up opportunities for people to meet on conference calls and when possible in person, is key.

The SURJ Basebuilding team is focused on growing the support for local organizing and among people dong this work in places around the country. One way we do this is by hosting regular national calls that feature local voices, offer lessons out of real on the ground stories, and share resources that support education and organizing. Topics emerge from the local work, from our people of color accountability relationships, and from our own observations based on what we are seeing as opportunities and challenges. Over the past three years, calls have included discussions of what Freedom Summer can teach us now, white people and immigration work, building your core leadership, how to start a group, rural organizing, and moving from talking to action.

SURJ Basebuilding helps not only by lifting up examples of local work we can all learn from, but by breaking the isolation among individuals, and among different efforts, state to state, city to city, or town to town. When the reality of oppression is underlined almost daily in the death of yet another Black person at the hands of police, and by the unprecedented marginalization of Black, Brown, and Native people, growing the sense that all our efforts add up to something matters a lot.

For example, several weeks ago, two of us from the Louisville SURJ (LSURJ) leadership collective met with four people from Henderson, a town in Western Kentucky. They wanted to talk about what they want to do and how SURJ can support them to begin organizing for racial justice. These four white, straight members of a United Church of Christ church there, one a former mayor of the town, had been part of the struggle for LGBTQIA equality in their town and recently were part of a reading group with Michelle Alexander's The New Jim Crow. We were able to share with them about SURJ and what others are trying to do around the country, and what we are doing in Louisville. They said that just affirming that what they are doing has meaning, and the fact that they can call on SURJ for resources and coaching, was a big help. A couple of their leaders were able to join the SURJ Basebuilding call about starting a SURJ affiliate group. To me, knowing that, in the small town of Henderson, Kentucky, twenty-one people recently came together to educate and take action for racial justice, is so exciting.

Dara Silverman: I love the way Carla and Pam McMichael (one of the other founders of SURJ and the Executive Director of the Highlander Center), talk about the founding of SURJ—because they speak about it as responding to the call from people of color but really committing to doing our own work with white people. I was just doing a training with Tema Okun, a longtime trainer and SURJ member in North Carolina, and in response to a question she said, "One thing I know for sure is I need to really love white people. To do this work we as white people really need to love and care for our white people." I feel that Tema articulated for me a big part of what is working in SURJ. Over the past two years especially, we have been successful at bringing more people into this work and building the tent of white people who see racial justice as a framework for their lives, relationships, and actions. We are living in a moment of huge opportunity and promise, but the question is, Will white people

"We need you defecting from white supremacy and changing the narrative of white supremacy by breaking white silence."

move into this challenge and be a part of a Black-led movement for liberation? More and more white people are saying yes—in the streets—from Baltimore, Maryland, to Charleston, South Carolina, from Dallas, Texas, to Urbana, Illinois.

Five days after the non-indictment of Darren Wilson, SURJ hosted a national call on taking action in solidarity with Ferguson. Eleven hundred people signed up and, with over six hundred people from around the country, it was an amazing opportunity to share information and offer clear ways that people in Ferguson were asking for white people to take action. For a few years, the SURJ Action Team had created toolkits to create and compile resources for white people to take actions on a range of issues. We had been in direct communication with folks on the ground from Ferguson Action, Black Lives Matter, the Anti-Racism Collective of the Justice Committee, and MORE. This was the first time we hosted a national call with steps for white people to take action. All of a sudden, we had people coming out of the woodwork wanting to work with us. We hosted a second call with Alicia Garza from Black Lives Matter and Maurice Mitchell from Ferguson Action. Alicia said to us, "We need you defecting from white supremacy and changing the narrative of white supremacy by breaking white silence."

Because of the work that SURJ had done—trainings around the country, creating accessible tools, and supporting groups through the Basebuilding team and mentorship—some people knew of our work. Because of the moment, a much bigger group was looking for support, and we had to set up the infrastructure and strengthen relationships on the ground to be able to respond quickly. In addition to the seventy-five groups SURJ is working with across the country, our trainings, the tool-kits we create, and the phone calls we host, SURJ has been approached by a number of movement organizations to find ways to support and develop their efforts to build a racial justice analysis into their work, their campaigns, and to develop deeper partnerships. From environmental groups like the Sierra Club and 350.org to religious groups including the United Methodist Women, the Presbyterian Diocese, and Transform; from parents groups across the country to college students to political groups like Moveon.org, Move to Amend, Southerners on New Ground (SONG), and the LGBT Task Force, the desire to more deeply engage and transform social justice organizations and movements is deep, urgent, and necessary. We also have a network of people, we call them SURJ Connectors (including Mutulu Olugbala [aka M1 from dead prez], Tim Wise, Piper Kerman, Paul Kivel, Debby Irving, Chris Crass, JLove Calderon, and many others) who are public figures, out in the world, who help spread the word about SURJ, connect folks to local groups, and encourage white people to plug in and take action.

Chris: How do you think about effectiveness and how do you measure it? Can you share an experience that helps you think about effective work in white communities for racial justice?

Sam: I think that it is necessary to look at the long term when thinking of effectiveness. Though there are moments of deep openings and mass shifts in consciousness, I believe that long-term transformation can also be slow and gradual. I understand effectiveness through the depths and durability of relationships that are built, as well as how well we are able to bring new folks into leadership. Opening up space for others to step into leadership, and building mutually supportive relationships with seasoned and new leaders, is the work that makes my heart beam and feels the most impactful for the long-term struggle. I believe that we must win concrete victories that change people's everyday lives. But if we do this without investing in each other as people and leaders, we won't be able to sustain our movement for the long term. I believe in celebrating campaign wins as well as moments when someone in our community moves deeper into leadership

Carla: If there are white people wanting to become active in challenging racism (and there are more and more every day), then I think part of measuring effectiveness has to be whether or not we are helping them engage. This means we need to be

"How are we supporting local groups of white people to listen and build trusting connections and partnerships with local communities of color?"

developing various ways, many ways, for people to be active in their local communities, and also in SURJ as a regional and national effort. This is an area we need more work on, and more learning from other effective organizing efforts. In the struggle to expand justice and make democracy real in this country, we have powerful examples of effective base building and organizing work. We have examples of white people defecting from white supremacy and joining people of color-led struggles for change. But there is not a lot of history of large enough numbers of white people rising up against racism in this country. So, part of this work, as the saying goes, is making the path as we are walking it.

One new project SURJ has undertaken that I am really excited about is outreach in white neighborhoods. We have just put out a call for white people to go door to door in white neighborhoods to have conversations with their neighbors about what is happening in Ferguson, in Baltimore, and in this country that denies opportunity, livelihood, and freedom to Black Americans. The conversation includes asking if we can put a Black Lives Matter yard sign in their yard. We hope this project will not only further train SURJ supporters in how to talk about race with other white people, and provide an experience for other white people to take a stand for Black lives, but identify racial justice supporters as well. This project, inspired by work already underway in St. Louis, and with the support of Black Lives Matter leaders, can be used to garner white support for local campaigns led by Black and other people of color against police violence, mass incarceration, disproportionate school suspensions, and more.

Dara: Coming out of a community organizing background, I was taught to measure effectiveness in concrete wins. Are we increasing the minimum wage? How much? How quickly? Part of my evolution as an organizer has been to move from a transactional framework towards a transformational framework. This means that it isn't just about what we win, how many actions we do, how much news coverage we get, but, What is the quality of the relationships? How are we supporting local groups of white people to listen and build trusting connections and partnerships with local communities of color? This looks different in Vermont then it does in Minneapolis.

"In order to end structural racism and to truly transform the world, we need everyone."

Some of the feedback we've gotten from our partnerships with Black leaders and groups is to go slow by respecting their decision-making process. I struggle with this individually, because of all my white training, but, ultimately, for us to be effective it is all about the relationships. This is why when we do trainings across the country, we base it in an organizing model of one-to-one conversations, relationship building, and connection. The need for belonging and connection for white people doing racial justice work is deep. A big part of making our work effective is supporting groups to build a local community, a culture, and take action from a basis of relationships. For example, we have a new SURJ chapter in Chicago. They've been meeting for months, going to actions, supporting the work of local people of color-led groups. They just co-sponsored their first action, a memorial for #RekiaBoyd and other Black women and girls who were killed by the police in Chicago.

Chris: What are the goals and strategies (as emergent, planned, messy, and sophisticated, basic as they may be) you're operating from?

Sam: In order to end structural racism and to truly transform the world, we need everyone. So white folks must be moved to challenge racism within ourselves, our communities, and the racist systems within which we live. I am invested in building strong infrastructure to support white racial justice organizing across the U.S. I have experienced the difficulty and isolation of doing this work in massively under-resourced areas, with a lack of models and mentors to look to for support and strategies. Several years ago, I was part of forming a white anti-racist organizing group in Tucson, Arizona, where the lack of resources for white people wanting to take leadership in organizing our own communities was discouraging. Through our affiliation with SURJ, we were able to connect with organizations around the country invested in similar kinds of work. I've found breaking isolation and sharing lessons across regions and movements to be crucial for building and sustaining the work, and in realizing that we are not starting from scratch. We are connected to larger histories of white people organizing against racism.

Much of our work in SURJ is creating space for these connections. For instance, recently someone working with a group of white people who work in primarily white environmental organizations in Alaska contacted us for support. We were able to connect him to an environmental justice organizer in New York state to talk about what folks in other places are doing within the environmental movement to address racism. Creating avenues for local leaders to share what's working, to strategize together, and to draw inspiration from each other helps strengthen all of our work.

Nashville SURJ First Public General Meeting. Photo: Andrew Krinks

Something we talk a lot about in SURJ is the strategy of connecting with our own mutual interest as white people with that of people of color in ending racism. I come from a Southern, working-class rural family. We are a people who have known in our bones what it means to struggle to live with dignity day-to-day. Yet, many people in my family are bound by deep racism, which strips them of their humanity and often pushes them to align against their own economic interests. It is in our direct interest to unite with other poor and working class folks, many of whom are people of color, to end racism and capitalism. I know that my people cannot get free unless we end white supremacy. So on both a soul and economic level, we have a mutual interest in ending systemic racism. Entering the struggle to organize other white people from this place has enabled me to connect with others on why we need to be in this fight for racial justice. If white folks understand what our stakes are in ending racism, we can build stronger relationships with each other, and can for a more deeply committed and invested base of white people to join the multiracial movement for justice

Carla: I love being asked about goals and strategies in a question with the word "messy" in it. For, indeed, the SURJ journey has been far from linear, or neat, or certain. We have big, broad goals like getting a critical mass of white people to break with

> **"...break with white supremacy, and become part of a people of color-led, multiracial movement for transformative change."**

white supremacy, and become part of a people of color-led, multiracial movement for transformative change. And we carry big broad questions around how we support the leadership of poor and working class white people, why that is critical, how we grapple with differences in this work, and how we really meet people where they are, not where we think they should be but aren't. And we have to create opportunities for white people to break silence and inaction in the face of racism and fight it, as white Southern Civil Rights activist and journalist Anne Braden said, "as if our lives depended on it, for in fact, they do." This takes a lot of steps that may seem small, like responding to a white activist beginning SURJ work in Dallas about how to do a white privilege conference (and connect it to action), to talking with someone in Bellamy, Oregon, to learn about their campaign for police accountability, or to encouraging a sister wanting to start something in southern Indiana.

Supporting, encouraging, and in some cases sparking local work to engage white people in racial justice is what we are doing. If we can be there for people trying to do this in spaces all over this country, it can add up to more than our individual parts, and more than just SURJ organizationally. The possibility, and indeed the hope, is that our numbers and impact, when joined with people of color-led efforts, can become a significant challenge to local, national, and indeed international expressions of U.S. white supremacy on the road to transformational change and collective liberation.

For Louisville SURJ, an example of this would be the campaign to expose and challenge the Cordish Company, notorious for racial profiling, worker abuse, and police harassment around the country. For over ten years, their Fourth Street Live! entertainment district in downtown Louisville got away with this, despite Black Civil Rights concerns. When Louisville SURJ formed, we were asked by those activists to help get Cordish's attention. By assembling a coalition that includes the ACLU of Kentucky, the LGBTQIA Fairness Campaign (both largely white base groups), and along with key leaders of color, LSURJ helped shine the light on Cordish racism, and pressure for change. We were able to leverage white privilege for anti-racism and suddenly the powers that be in Louisville government and corporate circles were paying attention.

Dara: Right now, we're really focused on the door-knocking efforts that Carla mentioned earlier. We see this as a great way to build the skills and capacity of the 40 local groups around the country that are participating. The skill and the muscle of being able to engage a wide swath of white people in motion—people who are recognizing that the system is rigged and are looking to put their efforts into taking action to transform the system into one which is not set up to privilege whiteness—is critical. We're in conversations with people from Black Lives Matter, Million Hoodies Movement for Justice, and other Black-led groups about the best ways to work together, and the role of SURJ as the biggest network of white people organizing white people to specifically engage other white people for racial justice in the U.S. We want to build the skills and capacity of all SURJ members and groups to be able to do outreach in white communities, to take principled stands with elected officials and the police, to shift culture through the arts, and to be arrested; and, to see all these tactics as part of a larger strategy to challenge the powers that perpetuate racial injustice, while to challenging and changing the political system locally, regionally, and nationally.

Another one of our principles within SURJ is that there is enough for all. One of the things that capitalism teaches us is a model of scarcity. It is a system that privileges the few at the expense of the many. We see part of the role of white people in racial justice work as bringing more resources into the movement. For each sign that a SURJ group buys, $1 goes to Black Lives Matter. Similarly, some of our groups are hosting fundraisers that benefit people of color-led organizing. From a house party in suburban Maryland to a walkathon/race being planned for this summer in Central Vermont, we believe that part of accountability is white people raising funds for people of color movement work. A lot of times white groups have more access to resources, and so we ask anyone who gives to SURJ to make an equal or greater gift to people of color-led organizing.

We are in conversations with our accountability council and an internal process exploring launching a campaign against police brutality and for community control of community resources. This would be our first national campaign, and it would be a real effort to reflect the multiple parts of SURJ, and to identify a campaign that can have local, regional, and national targets for change. The goal is not just legislative reform but what can lead to a transformation in the way we see safety in communi-

"Critical self-reflection and deep relationships of accountability with organizers of color are absolutely crucial for this work."

ties, and what it would look like to have neighborhood and city control of resources. Our planning for this will be grounded in conversation with our accountability partners in Black Lives Matter, the Movement for Black Lives more broadly, and with other people of color-led groups and organizations.

Chris: What challenges are you facing? How are you trying to overcome them? What are you learning from these experiences?

Sam: I see many white anti-racist groups struggling with moving beyond a small core and building a broad base. There is a lot of anxiety around prioritizing the work with other white people. I have felt a huge amount of shame about my whiteness, and in the past have tried to distance myself from "bad white people" to try to establish myself as a "good white person." Many of the people I determined were "bad white people" are members of my family and my home community, and this shame only heightened the distance between myself and my people—the people in my life with whom I relate to in some of the most deep and fundamental ways. If we can't hold our own communities together with love, how can we move forward together and transform the current oppressive and dehumanizing conditions?

On the national and local level, I've found that approaching this work with deep love for my people has been absolutely necessary for me to move through that shame, and has enabled me to connect with the people with whom I work in much deeper and genuine ways. At SURJ, we hold the value of calling people in, rather than calling people out. This means holding the tensions that arise in our differences, building deep relationships of trust and mutual respect, continuing to call people deeper into the work as they are, and challenging each other with love. This also means making sure that our spaces are accessible for everyone—in particular to people beyond what are often exclusive, activist circles.

Shame and fear-based culture is a huge barrier to organizing other white folks as well. Critical self-reflection and deep relationships of accountability with organizers of color are absolutely crucial for this work. Also, if we get stuck in our fear of making mistakes, we are doing a great disservice to ourselves and the larger movement.

As Maurice Mitchell said on one of our early calls about Ferguson, "Your anxiety about getting it right has nothing to do with Black liberation." The truth is that this work is often uncomfortable, and I believe that we need to take risks and push ourselves beyond our comfort zone. I am certain that we will make mistakes—we are not perfect and we are paving this road as we walk in many ways. I believe that accountability means continuing to show up, to keep coming back to the table with an open heart, and to build strength from the lessons that we learn from our mistakes.

Carla: One of the challenges we are facing is whether or not we are growing a culture of engagement in which we as white people can be in this not just today, but for the long haul, and not just as individuals, but as people who are growing collectively. We have to take on the issue of what is holding white people back, and not just chalk that up to white privilege, which, though part of it, is not the whole story. What if we could look at how we can engage white people from a place of welcome, support, and affirmation? What if we help each other through our mistakes, and are open about the fact that we all make them? What if we ground our commitment in the mutual interest we all have, people of color and white people, in joining together to fight for a society that values all of us? And what if we understand that no matter how nervous and unsure we are about how to take action, taking action is a core element of growing accountable relationships with people of color and people of color-led struggles?

SURJ is using what we are calling core organizing values to create a culture of white anti-racism work that helps people engage: Calling In, Taking Risks/Making Mistakes, Mutual Interest, and Accountability through Action. We use these values in our trainings, in our base-building work, and in the coaching we are doing with people around the country.

They resonate. It is as if people are hungry for a way to do this work that is uplifting, affirming, and values creativity—a way to do this work in which we can actually love one another through all our imperfection and, yes, our whiteness. Though we have been asked to do this work for decades by people of color, we remain uneasy with the idea that focusing on organizing other white people is actually a valuable, necessary thing we must do.

Here in Louisville, when, in response to the non-indictment in the police killing of Michael Brown, Black Lives Matter and Ferguson Action were asking for action at Department of Justice offices throughout the country, Louisville SURJ decided to answer that call. We conferred with local Black Lives Matter activists of color, and Louisville SURJ organized the rally.

Our focus was to reach out to white people to show up, and a large group did. At the same time, a largely people of color-led action disrupted business as usual at Metro City Hall. At a later point, the two actions joined each other and closed out together. One of the challenges for us in Louisville SURJ was whether or not it was okay for our white group to play a leadership role, and what that should look like. We were able to move through these challenges in an effective and accountable way, not only because of the cross-race relationships built long before this particular action, but based on our understanding that stepping into leadership in engaging other white people is what we need to be doing. When this question of whether or not there is a role for white leadership in this work festers, the conditions for uncertainty, hesitation, and inaction hold everyone back. But, and this is critical in this conversation, the white leadership we need is about engaging other white people, not about trying to take over people of color-led efforts, or organizing in communities of color. I think those of us who are white will make more progress on the very real and critical issues of accountability to people of color when we get clearer about showing up to organize other white people.

Dara: Our biggest challenges in SURJ right now are around capacity and moving members from talk into action. We've had such a huge growth in interest, engagement, and membership in the past nine months. We have jumped from being a fairly small, low to the ground network of 15 groups, to now more than 75 groups, multiple partnerships, and thousands of supporters and Facebook and Twitter followers. It is a huge leap. We know that history holds moments like this, and we've all been stretching to meet the needs of the time. For us to get to scale—where we can amplify our local organizing into an effective, national movement—is an exciting challenge to have in front of us.

As Carla and Sam talked about, a lot of our member groups get really stuck moving from the theory of opposing white supremacy to taking public action to engage other white people. Everyone is waiting for a leader of color to tell them or their group to take action. But here's the thing: we know that police brutality is wrong, we know that a black person is killed by the police (or some form of security forces) #Every-28Hours. This is why it is so crucial for all of us as white people to take action even knowing that we will make mistakes.

It's also been a real balancing act for me to fight my inclination to be engaging with SURJ members all the time. It's been crucial for me to set limits on my SURJ time, not plug my phone in in the bedroom—making time to exercise, grow food, meditate, and spend time with kids in my life. These practices are crucial for me to stay in this work for the long haul.

Chris: How are you developing your own leadership and the leadership of people around you to step up in these profound, painful, and powerful Black Lives Matter movement times?

Sam: Critical to my own development as an organizer has been mentorship and the development of deep relationships with other organizers who are in this work for the long haul. When I connected with SURJ, as well as with rural organizers in Oregon and from the South, I found a political and spiritual home. I was able to understand myself and my people as a part of a larger history. I was able to place myself within the legacy of anti-racist white Southern queers and women who dedicate their lives to the struggle for collective freedom. This connection grounds me. I find this grounding to be absolutely necessary to sustain long-term movement work.

As a young organizer, I find myself needing to constantly challenge myself to step up into leadership. I've struggled with self-confidence for my whole life, and it is really easy for me believe that other people can always do things better. When we were forming our organizing group in Tucson, we decided that it would be really important to start with a leadership development series, in order to build trust and shared political analysis with our core. I felt that I needed more training before I could lead something like that, but in Arizona, we don't have the same resources and training opportunities as there are in large cities with larger movement infrastructures. A small core of us planned a twelve week leadership development and organizing training that we facilitated ourselves, and out of that grew some really powerful immigrant rights solidarity work in Tucson. Through that experience I realized that some of the best learning comes from taking action and learning along the way. I have been learning to challenge myself and to step up, all while holding myself with love and understanding that I won't be perfect. Practicing self-love and continuing to come back to my love for my people and my deep desire for full liberation for everyone is what enables me to stay in the work and to grow with all of the beautiful folks that I move alongside in the struggle.

Dara: I am lucky to have had great mentors, co-workers, and fellow travellers over the past twenty years when I worked as a community organizer. I'm also lucky to have been studying somatics over the past four years with the Strozzi Institute and Generative Somatics. Somatics is a transformative practice that offers physical and emotional practices to help sustain and transform participants to be our most grounded selves. We're lucky in SURJ to be embarking on a movement partnership with Generative Somatics to train more than sixty of our leaders in 2016 in embodied leadership and organizing skills.

Carla: I will be forever grateful for the influence in my own journey of the Black Liberation movement, the liberation struggles against U.S. colonialism and imperialism, the labor movement, and other examples of people fighting for democracy, peace, and justice. I grew up in privilege, seeing from an early age that a very few people, including my own family, had too much, and so many people did not have enough. But as I opened my eyes and heart, I also discovered community, and a powerful legacy of resistance. I learned that when people organize collective power against oppressive systems, change can happen. From the artists—the poet activists like Mumia Abu-Jamal, Audre Lorde, and Mahmoud Darwish—I learned that the spirit must and can refuse all efforts to dehumanize us, and that when we each bring our gifts for the benefit of the whole, we all win. So for me, learning from the history of anti-oppression struggle, learning from the cultural activists and door-to-door organizers, is all critical to our own leadership development. Because of the way this helps me stay hopeful and focused, I want to share this with others. At the same time, I believe that the leaders we need most are leaders who see supporting others to lead as part of our own heartbeat, something we cannot live without. This means always developing structures that engage more rather than fewer people, building in ways that make various forms and levels of engagement possible, and being open to and curious about how people want to come into this work—the gifts we each bring. Only through collective action and collective leadership can we grow something we actually want and need to be part of. A collection of disconnected individuals or disconnected actions, no matter how "right" they may be, will not grow what is necessary for us to bring.

When we forget this, we are lost. When we remember this, and practice this, there is nothing that can stop the justice journey.

....

Sam Hamlin *is a community organizer and educator in Tucson, Arizona. She is currently the Volunteer Coordinator for Showing Up for Racial Justice (SURJ) and a member of the Tucson Solidarity Group.*

Carla F. Wallace *works to build justice community and collective leadership in Louisville, Kentucky, as part of Louisville Showing Up for Racial Justice, and as part of the national SURJ leadership and its Basebuilding Team.*

Dara Silverman *is the National Coordinator of SURJ and is based in Beacon, New York. Previously, she worked as a coach, consultant, yoga teacher, and community organizer. She supports leaders to be in the movement for the long haul.*

To learn more about Showing Up for Racial Justice, go to www.showingupforracialjustice.org.

Notes to a White Anti-Racist Group Organizing Community Discussions with White People About Black Lives Matter

Community Discussion on Racism and Racial Justice at the McElroy House Dardanelle, AR.
Photo: Meredith Martin-Moates

You asked about talking points to open these discussions. My suggestion, to help you prepare for the community discussions, is to first have a group conversation amongst yourselves as the leadership/planning team, on what helped open your eyes to these issues—what questions, what conversations really moved you. And then ask: What questions can we ask that will help open this space for conversation, learning, and vulnerability with other white people? And, in these events with people, it's really valuable for one or two of you who are leading it to share something about your own journey, about what's been hard and what's been rewarding and powerful. Sharing our own stories in honest and vulnerable ways opens space for others to do it as well—with the goal of making it a space for learning, rather than a space of judgment, competition, and guilt.

We need white folks engaged in this work to help illuminate the journey for other white people to go on—to speak to the journey so it isn't just terrifying, but also transformative in bringing us into beloved community. And white people, like everyone, we need leaders to help show the way, not dictate the way, but help white people see the possibilities of anti-racist work and get support to then find their way into it. And, in your stories, speak to how anti-racism has been a catalyst to be more powerful in working for collective liberation—how, for example, a world in which Black lives matter would be a better world for all of us.

The culture you create, the stories you can share, and questions that you think will be helpful for people—followed with concrete action steps that both support the Black Lives Matter movement and help other white people come into motion for racial justice—all need to help guide us into action, followed up with debriefs, asking, "How was that for you, what did you learn, and what can we draw from this experience to help us be more effective in our next action step?"

Notes to a White Anti-Racist Struggling with White Resistance in His Mostly White Church to Black Lives Matter

You and I and other white anti-racists need to believe in the potential of white people. But it will generally be a minority of white people who will move. For us, we need to develop an approach that does not expect support from other white people, but expects we must develop that support. This way, we aren't devastated by the lack of it; we can have more appreciation for (not take for granted) the support that is there and cultivate other white people's thirst to end white supremacy and develop their courage to work for racial justice.

So, for example, whenever you post something to a congregation/group Facebook page about racial justice, first ask three-to-six other white people in the community (who you know privately support or you think might support it) to be ready to post their support and share their own thoughts about what you post. This will help build momentum for racial justice, to practice asking others to step up, and to give other white people the opportunity to be on the right side of history. Try to let folks know, if they need support or have any questions, to let you know. And ask those folks who are supportive to join you in public demonstrations and community racial justice events to put consciousness into action.

Our goal as white anti-racists isn't to just challenge racism; it's significantly about building up other white people's anti-racist consciousness, commitment, and courage to act. And, again, not to expect it, as white supremacy trains white people to be compliant, supportive of, ignorant of, and enabling of white supremacy. As white anti racists we need to grieve this reality and set our minds on freeing other white people

"Our job as white anti-racists is to see that system, and then look for ways to help white people fight against it, to join beloved community."

from the poison of white supremacy by encouraging and supporting those we can to get involved; and, when we argue with the roadblock people, we do it to make them less effective, and with an eye towards the people who are witnessing this exchange, knowing they are usually the people we're actually trying to reach and move.

I encourage you and all of us who are white anti-racists to cultivate our skills at asking other white people to join us, not from guilt or shame, but from a thirst to overcome fear and be on the right side of history. White people, under white supremacist ruling class rule, were never meant to see Black people and other people of color as fully human. Our job as white anti-racists is to see that system, and then look for ways to help white people fight against it, to join beloved community.

And, in the meantime, to build your home base of people and community that nurture and feed you, to go back into the work—sometimes that's our church, and sometimes it isn't. Love to you.

"By the Strengths of All of Our Ancestors": An Interview with Dove Kent of Jews For Racial and Economic Justice in New York City

As New York City erupted in December 2015 in mass, nonviolent, disruptive direct action after the non-indictment of the officer who murdered Eric Garner, and the officers who were accomplices in this brutal crime, one of the actions that grabbed national headlines and many a heart was organized by Jews for Racial and Economic Justice (JFREJ). Over 400 members of JFREJ, including rabbis and other leaders in the Jewish community, took to the streets of the primarily white, wealthy, and Jewish Upper West Side. This civil disobedience was planned with their longtime partner organizations based in working class communities of color, and coordinating actions took place across the city.

Tears ran down my face as I followed the news, often with my three-year-old son nearby, of powerful, defiant, Black-life-affirming, white-supremacist-hegemony-defying marches, vigils, and large-scale direct actions igniting around the country after the Eric Garner non-indictment; and NYC was galvanizing us all. And JFREJ was a powerful force mobilizing a mainly, but not entirely, white Jewish base of members and supporters to be courageous for Black Lives Matter. I've long loved JFREJ, which began in 1990, and has been deeply committed to long-term multiracial organizing and campaigns to build people's power for collective liberation. As their mission statement reads, they are "inspired by Jewish tradition to fight for a sustainable world with an equitable distribution of economic and cultural resources and political power."

JFREJ Mass Direct Action for Eric Garner, New York City, NY. Photo: Simone Zimmerman

I knew that JFREJ's actions in December were part of a years-long campaign against police violence in working class communities of color, and that with their vision, strategy, organizing experience, infrastructure, and leadership, they could offer insights and lessons for many of us around the country who are asking, "How do we help carry the momentum of these mass action times into long-term campaigns to win structural change?" Dove Kent, the executive director of JFREJ, shares from their organizational experience to help us think about that question.

Chris Crass: How are you working to move white people into the racial justice movement in this time? What's working? And what are you learning from what works?

Dove Kent: Inspired by the strengths of all of our ancestors, we organize against racism from a Jewish perspective. Jews engage with whiteness in complex ways. Anti-racist organizing from a Jewish perspective must begin with the diversity of our own experiences: JFREJ's membership encompasses the multicultural breadth of our community, including Mizrahi, Sephardi, Ashkenazi, and Black and Latina/o Jews. Some Jews may engage with Black Lives Matter as white allies, while others bring their insights and experiences as Jews of color. White Jews may often engage with whiteness through diasporic family histories and immigrant memories, alongside their

Jewish Leaders and Community Engage in Defiance for BLM. Photo: Simone Zimmerman

current lived experiences of race privilege in the United States. For white Jews, our anti-racist work begins with ourselves—through deconstructing racialization and whiteness in ourselves and our community, and fighting against white supremacy in our organization, our movement, and our city.

At JFREJ, we're currently working to move white people into racial justice work in ways that will last beyond this current movement moment. The Black Lives Matter movement has mobilized people across the country, and their energy has inspired many white Jews to get involved in our police accountability campaign and other anti-racism work in New York City. We want to make sure that we're training and organizing these hundreds of new members for the long haul, so they don't abandon this necessary work when the mainstream media moves on.

Because of the trust and accountability we've built with organizations led by people of color, poor and working class, and immigrant communities over the last twenty-five years, we've been able to mobilize white people into bold action and to take strategic risks in our work. In that time, our community has learned that relationships built on trust and commitment are the most important element of our work, and that these relationships are cultivated through consistent and accountable action. Over months and years, we show up with our partners for campaign planning meetings, actions, and press conferences, but also as volunteers for their events, donors at their fundraisers, and for jail support when they get arrested. So, when opportunities arise for strategic, visible action led by white members of our organization—whether that's a civil disobedience, a public demonstration, a meeting with city council members, or a media campaign—we take those opportunities head-on. Our partners trust us to bring the same level of rigor and accountability to the action we lead as we bring to the action we support.

A helpful accountability mechanism we use before taking action is to ask ourselves two questions: For the sake of what? and, Who will this benefit? When we're working in deep connection and alignment with our partner organizations and the larger movement against anti-Black racism, we show up better with each other. Being in the struggle together—with our bodies, our minds, and our resources—grounds us in what is most important. The moments when we have had to rely on each other (for jail support, for security at marches and protests), have helped us feel connected to each other and loosened the sense of isolation and alienation many of us grew up with because of racism and classism. As a community, JFREJ demonstrates that we are in this fight for the long haul.

Chris: How are you developing your own leadership and the leadership of people around you to step up in these profound, painful, and powerful Black Lives Matter movement times?

Dove: Our goal is to empower directly targeted constituencies to bring their experience, expertise, and vision to bear on the direction of the movement. We're investing deeply in new base building and leadership development at all levels of the organization. We're working to center the leadership of Jews who are on the local and global "front lines" of resistance to racism, colonization, displacement, and erasure—specifically Jews of Color, Mizrahi and Sephardic Jews, and poor and working class Jews.

At the same time, we're continuing to leverage the race and class privilege of some of our members in powerful organizing work. We believe that modeling a multiracial, multi-ethnic, cross-class, intergenerational community committed to social justice is a powerful tool to shift the broader Jewish community towards justice.

We're continuing to support the leadership development of our staff and members situated at the intersection of whiteness and Jewishness. Developing my own leadership and the leadership of the white Jews around me in this time has required a strong focus on countering isolation and individualism. Whiteness teaches us that our sense of self-worth is based on excelling as individuals, which can lead us away from long-term commitments to movement building. For those white people who grew up middle class or rich (like me), we also got the message that depending on other people was a kind of failure. This illusion of independence is built on the very invisibility of countless workers and care-takers in our stories and our lives. Alongside white JFREJ staff and white members, I struggle daily to cut through these messages of individualism and this isolation. For me, that has meant a daily practice of recognizing for myself and demonstrating for others—particularly white Jews—just how much I need them. It means showing vulnerability and not having all the answers. It also means recognizing the long history of anti-racism organizing that has come before us, honoring those ancestors and that lineage to which we belong, and laying groundwork for those activists who will come after us. Leadership development in this moment of profound movement building against anti-Black racism has meant cutting through the lies that white supremacy tells us, and learning and relearning how to build connection and our sense of belonging.

At JFREJ, we strive to do our work from this place of love and connection. The bonds we make with our partner organizations are called "coalitions," but really they grow out of our refusal of the illusion of independence that we're taught under

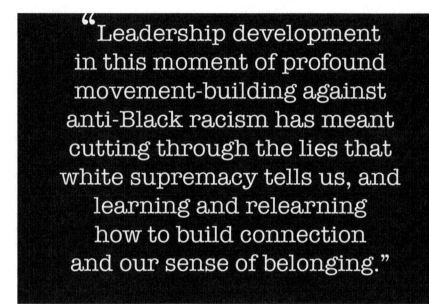

"Leadership development in this moment of profound movement-building against anti-Black racism has meant cutting through the lies that white supremacy tells us, and learning and relearning how to build connection and our sense of belonging."

white supremacy. Our work itself asks the question: When we confront and resist whiteness and "independence," and center the voices and the leadership of people of color, what can shift inside us and between us?

JFREJ is offering trainings for white Jews to:

- provide a practical framework and action steps to practice accountable anti-racism, create trusting multiracial spaces, and keep building a powerful racial justice organization and movement;

- support white Jews to come to a common understanding of the ideology of white supremacy, the practice of American racism, and the assimilation of many Jews into whiteness—and to situate ourselves and our community within that context and history;

- provide a shared language and a shared analysis of accountability and anti-racist practice specific to Jewish institutions, so we can understand and accept certain ground rules for our relationships with people of color, and specifically Jews of color within our organization;

- counter isolation and practice connection and interdepedence in all forms of our work.

Anti-racism is really a lifelong struggle, so we work with our membership to build a new way of seeing our lives, making a long-term commitment to each other and our work.

Chris: How do you think about effectiveness and how do you measure it? Can you share an experience that helps you think about effective work in white communities for racial justice?

Dove: We try to work with both urgency and patience. We think about effectiveness in three-to-ten-year increments, and we measure it in cultural shifts as well as more directly measurable results such as policy change and effective implementation. We've learned from our organization's history that it can take up to ten years to pass anti-racist legislation or win other battles for concrete changes to the political and social landscape.

For example, JFREJ organized from 2002 to 2010 in support of Domestic Worker organizations—led by Caribbean, South Asian, Latina, and African American women—to pass the New York Domestic Workers Bill of Rights, the first statewide legislation in the country to include domestic workers under labor protections. Over that nine-year period, we worked within Jewish communities to raise awareness, build leadership, and organize employers of domestic workers, synagogues, and community members in the fight for equitable pay, benefits, respect, dignity, and justice for domestic workers. Through this campaign, we also built the organizing skills, political analysis, and capacity of our members, our synagogue partners, rabbis, and Jewish communities to fight for and win campaigns for racial justice in New York. Since 2010, we've continued to organize individual Jews and Jewish institutions to ensure the effective implementation of the law.

JFREJ has also been working with our partners to fight against police brutality for nearly two decades, so the recent upsurge in movement work across the city and country is deeply inspiring. In today's fight, we're using multiple tactics that confront the violence of whiteness through the strategic use of public space and media, and the resilient insistence upon cultivating allyship. One effective tactic we recently under-

JFREJ Action for Eric Garner.
Photo: Simone Zimmerman

took was civil disobedience on New York's (primarily white, wealthy, and Jewish) Upper West Side to protest the non-indictment of the officers responsible for Eric Garner's murder. The action involved about four hundred JFREJ members and was done in collaboration with our partner organizations, led by Justice Committee, mobilizing in other neighborhoods that same night. Our goal at JFREJ was to take up space in public and move the conversation about police brutality into white Jewish communities and other white communities.

We succeeded in getting covered by every major national and local Jewish press outlet, in addition to many non-Jewish national and local media (and quite a few Jewish local papers outside of New York). White Jewish leaders across the city increased their engagement, and have continued to be a part of the conversation. The action has helped us to successfully mobilize rabbis and other Jewish leaders into subsequent tactics. Many of the national Jewish publications that had not previously printed articles on police accountability finally began to discuss this issue, making their readers face the subject of state/police violence against Black people. This coverage also brought widespread recognition of anti-racist movements to the mainstream Jewish press. We recognize, of course, that this tactic did not result immediately in a change in policing practices in New York City. But it has led to broader coverage of police violence, a significant rise in mainstream Jewish awareness, and an invigorated engagement with police accountability efforts over the subsequent months.

Chris: What are the goals and strategies (as emergent, planned, messy, and sophisticated, basic as they may be) you're operating from?

Dove: We believe that fighting to win real change means growing movements and campaigns too strong to be ignored. So we're building our power by building a robust base of members. We're developing and supporting leaders, forming and supporting coalitions, and waging strategic campaigns to win systemic change in New York City.

As we organize in multiple spheres to transform systems of economic and racial injustice, we simultaneously transform the consciousness of the people who participate in organizations and movements, as well as the organizers themselves. We seek to make change that will last beyond any one issue campaign or election and will not sacrifice long-term outcomes for short-term gains.

We're currently working in deep partnership with organizations led by communities of color to end "broken windows" policing, both through legislative reform and cultural change. In the last few years, we've joined in coalition with Communities United for Police Reform and alongside some of our long-term partners like the Justice

Committee, Committee Against Anti-Asian Violence: Organizing Asian Communities, and the Arab American Association of New York. In 2013 we celebrated a victory when the New York City Council passed the Community Safety Act, establishing permanent oversight of the NYPD and protections against identity-based profiling. Our coalition is now organizing to pass the Know Your Rights Act, which would end the practice of unconstitutional searches and require police to identify themselves during stops. This will be another step towards building the power of targeted communities in relationship to the police.

On the cultural front, we're leading "Know Your Responsibilities" trainings for New Yorkers not targeted by the NYPD. The trainings demonstrate how to observe, record, intervene, and offer support to fellow New Yorkers when they're harassed by the NYPD. Our goal is to develop new understandings of safety among white New Yorkers and to build a culture of accountability in our communities. These trainings were developed as a supplement and companion to the People's Justice's Copwatch "Know Your Rights" trainings, which give tools to people who are targeted by the police—specifically people of color—to protect themselves from abusive policing practices. By teaching white residents how to reach out to their fellow New Yorkers during police encounters, we're demonstrating the kind of community we want to build and creating a culture shift with our allies and neighbors. As our trainers say, "Everyday copwatching is that radical and mundane act of watching out and caring for each other."

We're also creating opportunities for really exciting cross-pollination and development of cultural work between our members and our partners. We know that successful social movements advance through embodied critical thought and the culture shifts that come from exploring resistance with all of our senses and traditions. We're committed to teaching each other and studying and creating with our allies.

Chris: What challenges are you facing? How are you trying to overcome them? What are you learning from these experiences?

Dove: While we are working to transform our organization to center the leadership of targeted communities, we are still years behind where we need to be to truly embody anti-racist, anti-classist practice.

JFREJ started taking concrete action two years ago to create change in our organization. We decided to invest deeply in emerging leaders from marginalized constituencies within our community. We are working to ensure that these members, particularly Black Jews, are positioned to lead Jewish social justice work, rather than haphazardly being fit into support roles. We are steadily developing clearer thinking and principles to guide this transformation, and experiencing progress, but we recognize how much we still have to learn and build.

JFREJ Action for Eric Garner.
Photo: Simone Zimmerman

We are slowly growing the capacity of our own organization and the wider Jewish community to embrace racial justice as a Jewish priority that directly impacts our Jewish brothers and sisters, and we're investing time, energy, and resources in bold action and movement-building at the Jewish grassroots. We are hopeful that we as a multiracial Jewish community will rise to this immediate and long-term challenges.

Funding this work is a challenge. Institutional funders often see this kind of work as an "internal" project rather than as a major challenge to white supremacy in the Jewish community and beyond. We have learned that in order to be the kind of laboratory of innovation and resistance we need to be, we have to fund this work ourselves through the grassroots—our members. Thankfully, the JFREJ membership is taking up this challenge and supporting the organization in bold and inspiring ways.

....

Dove Kent *is the Executive Director of Jews For Racial and Economic Justice (JFREJ) in New York City. Dove comes to JFREJ with ten years of experience in issue-based, identity-based, and neighborhood-based organizing in Boston and St. Louis. Dove gives thanks to Leo Ferguson, Anna Torres, Amanda Altman, Purvi Shah, Christopher Messinger, and Julie JD Davids for their help with the interview.*

To learn more about Jews for Racial and Economic Justice, go to www.jfrej.org.

Notes to a Veteran White Anti-Racist Activist on Cynicism as New White People Join the Movement for Black Lives Matter

I hear you on that initial reaction of not trusting new people, and wondering where they were before, but crisis is when new energies are unleashed and new people are seeing things and experiencing things for the first time and their consciousness and commitments are shifting. It's often in crisis, like the Black Lives Matter movement times we're in, when large numbers of people, of all backgrounds, previously inactive, get active. You don't have to trust new people, but we have a responsibility to find ways of helping and supporting new people to get involved in helpful ways. It is not that we have to hold everyone's hands and lose momentum as each person is in their process, but rather to see that new people, generally speaking, genuinely want to do the right thing, and this is a moment to help them do that.

We can't close the door on new people, or doubt their commitment because they weren't here before. Quite simply, we would never grow, and would become more like a club than a movement if we did. Our responsibility is to remember the moments when we were new, when our consciousness shifted, when we tried to get involved, and then try to do the things that others did that helped us and try to improve on what others did that either sucked or just didn't work.

❝...we need you.❞

Thank you for the years you have put into the work, and while I agree we need pragmatism born of things not going well, we must guard against cynicism. It is the cancer of the ruling order eating away possibility and hope in the spirits of liberation-loving people. This doesn't mean trusting everyone; rather, it means having good boundaries on trust, so that we can keep our eyes on the prize and stay focused on what can be done, rather than getting stuck on what can't. It also means having a realistic and hopeful sense of what is possible in these times—to both step up in powerful and helpful ways, and grow individually into the kind of liberation leaders we need. And we need you.

Notes to a White Activist Working in a Majority White Multi-Issue Group, Getting Push Back from the White Director About Making Racial Justice a Focus of the Organization's Social Media

That's great you talked with lots of people in your organization after the director said others agreed with their concern about how much you're focusing on racial justice. And it's great that they all expressed support for what you're putting out in the organization's social media on racial justice. Now it's time to help mobilize that private support into public/organizational support.

Have conversations with some of the folks in your organization who say they support you, and help build up your shared politics and perspective by asking for their thoughts on how anti-racism helps move the mission statement of the organization/ the work and values of the organization forward. Particularly for white people, they are rarely asked these kinds of questions, so this is about helping build up anti-racist muscle to push down the barriers to your organization having strong racial justice politics and practice.

And then ask some of them to speak to the director with the concerns, and ask them to share why they think this is how the organization can fulfill its purpose in the community. You want to try to avoid this becoming a personal issue between you and the director, and you want to build up the support in the organization for this work, so asking people to step up like this can be helpful on both accounts.

When talking with your director, assume they are coming from a good place. Ask them questions, like, "What are you afraid will happen? Why do you think we'll lose support in the community?" and then ask the director about times in the past when the organization built up support for what was seen as highly controversial, and how this is part of what the organization celebrates about its history and how this is an opportunity to be leaders helping people in the community be their best for justice, rather than letting "our own" fear and the "projected fear of others" dictate the agenda.

Perhaps share some of your own process of being a white person afraid to speak up, but why you do it, and the positive changes you've seen as a result. The key is to not trap the director in the position of being oppositional to racial justice and your work, but try to have conversations where you're affirming the director's desire to do good work, and try to help show how racial justice, particularly in these times of the Black Lives Matter movement, is the way for the organization to live its mission and rock it.

That said, my advice is to prioritize building active support with staff who are most receptive, and then other staff who seem open, as well as members and supporters in the broader community who you have affinity with, trying to get as many folks who have organization influence on board as you can, while also having these conversations with your director. To the best of your ability, try to stay in the position of being a leader building up your community's capacity to be awesome for racial justice and try to diminish the possibility of this just becoming an antagonistic relationship between you and your director that gets locked into a dynamic in which neither of you can be your best selves and you can't do the work you want to do.

Counter-protest at Confederate Rally in Hillsborough, NC. Photo: David Neal

"Which Side Are You On?": An Interview with Liz Perlman and Seth Newton Patel of AFSCME Local 3299 on Organizing in the Labor Movement for Black Lives Matter

While the long history of racism in the labor movement is often used as an example of how the ruling class divides working people, and how workers racialized as white have fought for access to white privilege at the expense of workers of color, the labor movement is also rich with multiracial, anti-racist, racial justice campaigns, lessons, and victories that have built working class power for economic justice for all. These efforts have overwhelmingly been led by working class people of color, and white anti-racist workers are also an important part of this history and contemporary struggle.

This interview is with white racial justice union leaders and organizers Liz Perlman and Seth Newton Patel. In response to the Black Lives Matter movement, a multiracial group of worker leaders and the board of the union and staff, with Black workers at the forefront, started up the Racial Justice Working Group to build solidarity with the Black Lives Matter movement and move racial justice forward in the union for the long haul.

Chris Crass: How are you working to move white people into the racial justice movement in this time? What's working? And what are you learning from what works?

Liz Perlman and Seth Newton-Patel: AFSCME Local 3299 is a union of over 22,000 patient care and service workers at the University of California's (UC) hospitals and campuses. Our own constitution reminds us that "our legacy goes back to . . . the fight to end slavery, the Civil Rights movement, and lives on today as we seek fairness for all working families and respect for new immigrant workers." With a union that is nearly eighty percent people of color (of those, approximately thirteen percent Black), we are currently working to move our multiracial membership—including our white workers who make up approximately seventeen percent of our union—to support racial justice movements primarily through the creation and campaigns of our union's Racial Justice Working Group (RJWG).

The RJWG was born of our Local's elected worker leaders' individual involvement in the Black Lives Matter (BLM) movement. After multiple conversations with Black executive board members—including one with a board member who had just returned from a BLM action with his nephew in Arizona—our president, Kathryn Lybarger, formed the RJWG in December of 2014. Lybarger invited any and all executive board members to participate, and specifically encouraged Black members to join. Some leaders brought a wealth of past experience, including one member who had completed the C. L. Dellums African American Leadership School. Black, Latino, and white leaders joined the committee, and Local union staff were also invited to participate in supporting the work of the RJWG.

The RJWG's first goal was to educate and involve our union's top worker leadership—a 40-member statewide executive board—to stand in solidarity with the BLM movement and struggle against police brutality by doing more than just passing a resolution. We asked our white and Latino worker leaders to play an active role in an internal campaign led by a predominantly Black committee. We asked Steven Pitts to share his expertise in Black worker organizing and education—his regular feedback informs our RJWG's vision, and he facilitated our first board training.

Labor Against Police Brutality March Oakland, CA. Photo: Brooke Anderson

At the first training worker leaders were asked to share what the movement for Black lives has meant to them, how AFSCME's involvement in the Civil Rights movement strengthened our union, and how racism is used by the UC to divide us, as well as how racism operates within our union. While most appreciated the history and context, board members' reactions ranged from being deeply inspired to showing indifference. We found that connecting the BLM movement to our union's history and UC's anti-union tactics were particularly effective in convincing white and other non-Black leaders to actively participate in the conversation. During our RJWG debrief, our committee observed that while the training was a good beginning, we had a long way go.

Inspired by Pitts to create a "culture of conversation" about racism in our union and workplaces, our committee set out to organize our board, followed by our hundreds-strong statewide worker leadership structure. The RJWG's next training will be held at our statewide worker leadership conference this summer, after which our committee plans to launch an internal campaign to systematically collect and share our members' stories of police violence and racism. Ultimately we aim to use our internal campaign to fuel broader AFSCME 3299 action in support of the BLM movement and to contribute to struggles for racial justice at UC.

In addition to internal education and organizing, our leaders have also been inspired by efforts of other San Francisco Bay Area unions. For example, ILWU Local 10 shutdown the Port of Oakland on May Day and marched with other unions to City Hall. The Alameda Labor Council disinvited Alameda County District Attorney Nancy O'Malley (originally selected as the Labor Council's "Woman Warrior of the Year") from its annual awards celebration. She had refused to drop charges against the Black Friday 14 protesters whose civil disobedience action stopped BART train service in November. While not at all an exhaustive list, Fight for $15, SEIU 1021, UNITE HERE locals, and AFSCME United Domestic Workers have regularly participated in BLM actions. San Francisco Jobs with Justice recently organized a "Black Lives Matter at Work" panel made up of Black labor leaders to beg the question: What would our labor movement look like if Black lives mattered?

As white labor leaders, we have found that we have the responsibility to create space, drive, and resources for ongoing racial justice education and organizing. We have learned that we have to keep focus on the specificity and stories of anti-Black racism, meaningfully acknowledge police violence against other communities of color, and give white workers a vision for what we stand to gain in the fight for racial justice. We are learning from several board conversations on the BLM movement that we must be better prepared to respond to comments from non-Black leaders—members from white, Latino, and Asian communities—that can serve to diminish the devastating reality of police violence against Black communities. And, most of all: we are learning that our work within our union and labor movement has just begun.

Chris: How do you think about effectiveness and how do you measure it? Can you share an experience that helps you think about effective work in white communities for racial justice?

Liz and Seth: Our union generally thinks about effectiveness as the ability to build power in the UC system—and for our labor movement—that can make meaningful change and lift up the lives of working people, primarily through the recruitment and development of a representative and massive organization of worker leaders committed to collective action. With this foundation, we see effectiveness at moving our Local to contribute to struggles for racial justice as: our ability to educate and organize our worker leadership and membership to see how the fight for racial justice is part of our fight for economic justice. Ideally, this will make our economic justice campaigns inseparable from campaigns for racial justice at UC, and inspire Local 3299 leadership to actively participate in the BLM movement. A further measure of effectiveness would be our union's ability to collaborate with other

AFSCME Local 3299 Racial Justice Group.
Photo: Monica DeLeon

unions and community-based worker organizations across California to further expand labor movement support for the BLM movement.

To get anywhere close to these ambitious goals, of course, we must create many modest markers along the way. Our RJWG currently aims to engage our board and member leadership in a series of racial justice trainings, teach worker leaders how to talk to and move their co-workers to support our union's racial justice organizing, and have a larger presence at Black Lives Matter actions.

Multiple members of the RJWG remind us: while we are off to an encouraging start with a multiracial conversation, we have work to do facilitate deeper commitment. During our RJWG debrief meeting following the first board training, one Black committee member said: "I didn't see any white folks speaking. I was reading their faces and their body language, and it looked like they couldn't wait for it to be over. There were certain people that I'm looking at and I'm thinking: you really don't have anything to say?" At the same time, this RJWG leader said he felt that "it's been a blessing to have this topic discussed openly on the floor," and looked forward to the next training that would provide additional tools for having organizing conversations with non-Black members.

Chris: What are the goals and strategies (as emergent, planned, messy, and sophisticated, basic as they may be) you're operating from?

Liz and Seth: Aside from the goals and strategy already discussed, we have set out to drive an internal education and storytelling campaign using our union's history and worker leaders' own personal stories. The 1968 Memphis Sanitation Workers Strike is the most celebrated example of AFSCME support for racial justice, and the starting point for many internal conversations about how economic and racial justice struggles are truly inseparable. Thirteen-hundred Black sanitation workers went on strike to fight Memphis' racist response after the deaths of two workers crushed by a malfunctioning truck. They joined AFSCME Local 1733. Martin Luther King 'Jr. was assassinated while mobilizing support for the strikers, the day after delivering his "I've Been to the Mountaintop" speech to those workers. In our first board training, Steven Pitts presented a video documenting the struggle, moving multiple board members to tears.

> **"In addition to using our union's history, we find that our own worker leaders' telling of personal stories of police violence is a powerful way to move other workers."**

We have also recently undertaken an effort to gather and share the history of our own Local's relationship to struggles for racial justice at UC. In 1970, sixty-five Black residence hall maids at UC Berkeley organized to join an AFSCME local that had originally been chartered at UC Berkeley back in 1948. Race and gender discrimination were as big an issue as the maids' low wages, and other unions, the Black community, and students actively participated in support. We still have more to learn about this and other struggles to both use them effectively and do them justice. In addition to using our union's history, we find that our own worker leaders' telling of personal stories of police violence is a powerful way to move other workers. Each RJWG leader has had numerous, powerful stories to share; even non-Black members, with coaching, could come to identify examples of how police violence targets Black communities, in turn negatively impacting all working class people. We believe in leading—but not stopping—with the stories of Black worker leaders. We expect that building stronger Black-Brown alliances—as well as white worker leadership against white supremacy—will require that non-Black workers also participate in the story-telling. Our RJWG is currently coming up with an internal campaign to systematically collect, document, and distribute our members' experiences with police violence. We hope that the collection and sharing of these stories will enable systematic organizing conversations and ultimately recruitment for racial justice campaigns.

Chris: What challenges are you facing? How are you trying to overcome them? What are you learning from these experiences?

Liz and Seth: Many. We are challenged when worker leaders remain unconvinced by our explanations of why our Local should be involved in the BLM movement. When it seems as though our methods—use of AFSCME's history, worker leaders' personal stories, the ways in which UC management divides our membership based on race, or our vision for a more powerful labor movement—do not move members, we hope that tenacity and the willingness to engage in ongoing one-on-one conversations will lead to breakthroughs.

We are challenged because police unions are a part of our labor movement, and many AFSCME affiliates represent law enforcement officers. A month after Michael Brown was killed, AFL-CIO president Richard Trumka spoke openly about this challenge. He said, "The reality is we still have racism in America. Now, some people might ask me why our labor movement should be involved in all that has happened since the tragic death of Michael Brown in Ferguson. And I want to answer that question directly. How can we not be involved? Union members' lives have been profoundly damaged in ways that cannot be fixed... Our brother killed our sister's son." Trumka referred to the fact that both Michael Brown's mother and killer are union members.

We need to be deliberate about engaging with AFSCME affiliates representing law enforcement around issues of policing, profiling, sentencing, and reentry. One initial step in this direction was our Local's effort to organize AFSCME support for the sentencing reform Proposition 47 passed by voters in 2014—reducing nonviolent drug possession and petty theft crimes from felonies to misdemeanors. The only AFSCME affiliate opposing the proposition—the Los Angeles Probation Department Union,

AFSCME Local 685—was not convinced that there would be adequate funding to address the workload increase that would result from sentencing reform.

AFSCME Staff at BLM March Oakland, CA. Photo by Brooke Anderson

Finally, it is a challenge to maintain focus and capacity to support the RJWG's internal education and organizing alongside ongoing union contract, enforcement, non-union organizing, and political and leadership development campaigns pulling us in many directions at once. While we do not have easy answers to this enduring challenge, we are also working to (1) incorporate a racial justice analysis in our ongoing campaigns—such as our fight for a community benefits agreement for the planned UC Berkeley Global Campus at Richmond Bay, and our campaign to in-source contract workers across the UC system, and (2) develop the leadership of our RJWG members.

Chris: How are you developing your own leadership and the leadership of people around you to step up in these profound, painful, and powerful Black Lives Matter movement times?

Liz and Seth: To develop our own leadership and that of our RJWG, we check in one-on-one; we recruit RJWG members to take leadership roles of co-chairing the committee, driving our vision, and participating as trainers. Our executive vice president and RJWG member, Michael Avant, has stepped up to provide more leadership. We also ask seasoned labor leaders outside of our own union to share their experience and feedback. We pay attention to the research and recommendations of Black labor leaders, such as those in the Discount Foundation's report, "Black Workers Matter,"[1] and the Institute for Policy Studies' "And Still I Rise: Black Women Labor Leaders' Voices, Power, Promise."[2]

Yet in the wake of the devastating white terrorist attack killing nine Black people at the Emanuel African Methodist Episcopal Church in Charleston—only the latest example of the ongoing, sanctioned violence against Black people at home, play, worship, and work—we are reminded that we white labor leaders have so far to go in developing our leadership and the leadership of those around us to step up for racial justice. Fortunately, we get to draw from the courageous, creative, and visionary Black Lives Matter leadership and action all around us.

....

Liz Perlman *is the executive director of AFSCME 3299 and a mother.*

Seth Newton Patel *is Local 3299's lead negotiator, father of two, and author of "Have We Built the Committee? Advancing Leadership Development in the U.S. Labor Movement," which appeared in the March 2013 issue of WorkingUSA. For more on AFSCME 3299's past and present campaigns, see "Strikes Win Staffing Protections at University of California" in Labor Notes.*

To learn more about AFSCME Local 3299, go to www.afscme3299.org.

---

1. To read the report and learn more, visit: www.discountfoundation.org/blackworkers matter.
2. Also visit www.and-still-i-rise.org.

Notes to a Comrade on Using the Buddy System to Bring New People in and Build Up a Local Anti-Racist/ CollectiveLiberation Organization

Using the buddy system to pair up existing members with new members is a mechanism to bring in new people, build capacity and build momentum.

Goals:

1. Support new members to become familiar with the history, purpose, politics, relationships/alliances/accountability, direction, decision-making process, and expectations of being part of the group.

2. Have a one-on-one system of support for new people with the hope that this can help them step up in ways that are actually helpful to the momentum of the group as opposed to opening big questions that are already resolved. Ask questions of them and yourself: "Should white people really be stepping up in these ways? Who are we accountable to?" Support the development of the new person to be part of the group and respect the work the group has already done, the decisions it has made, and the path it has followed up to this point. Yes, we want new people to help make the road, but it's useful for the new person to know they are on a particular road to begin with.

3. Support relationship building between experienced members and new members to help build the power of the group. Fulfill its goals and objectives through supporting relationship-based group cohesion, health, and community.

4. Allow the experienced person develop their own leadership by supporting a new person coming into the organization. This often means the experienced person getting the opportunity to speak about the group's big-picture vision, politics, history, purpose, and culture, and, in the process, hopefully, the experienced person learns to take more responsibility and feel more ownership over the group. For this reason, it's important to pay attention to who is being a buddy, and to help lots of different people play this role, as it is an important leadership function and leadership development opportunity.

5. There may be initial pushback to the layer of formality and work a buddy system brings. Those who have been involved in grassroots organizations know that— while there are honeymoon periods of struggle, during which people feel the unity and power of being in the streets together—there are also many opportunities for group dysfunction to emerge. While the buddy system won't eliminate group dys

function, it can front-load support work to help the group be more effective in accomplishing external and internal goals, and try to use foresight to overcome commonplace problems. It also helps remind the group that relationships, trust, and culture are key to moving forward. The system also helps the group culture be literate about the group's reasons for existing, its history, its politics, and its purpose for being. Being able to feel and function like a team with shared values and shared objectives is the goal.

Implementation:

1. Invite someone to a one-on-one meeting for a walk or coffee to go over these things, and get to know each other. A good buddy should ask questions so as to be able to come away from such a meeting with a deeper sense of the new person's heart and reasons for wanting to do this work and be part of this group, and with a sense of helpful suggestions to offer the person in their coming into the group.

2. Check in after the first few meetings with a text or email just to see how it was for the person. Give them feedback if appropriate, like, "I think it was really good when you asked that clarifying question," or "That's awesome you stepped up to help move some logistics forward. Let me know if questions come up, and remember you can ask people for help; we're a team." This will help nourish a positive, affirming culture that gets things done. You're not a club; you're a political organization with goals and you want to build a team and community, as comrades.

3. Challenges do come up. People will bring sexist or classist dynamics in. Some will take initiative outside the group that isn't helpful, or will be hardline about the group going in a different direction than where people have been trying to go. Folks won't agree with the person. Have a buddy who already has a relationship of accountability, and check in about it and give honest feedback to them. Help them grow and help the group grow.

4. Affirm when you see the person rocking out after a few months, and acknowledge it: "It's great the way you've become part of the group, and are here are three things you've done that really made an impact on our team." Give them positive examples and feedback if there have also been challenges. After this, the buddy relationship will end formally, with both of you now being members of the group with a closer relationship as a result.

This is how I've seen it implemented in the San Francisco Bay Area-based Heads Up Collective which I was a member of, and in other groups around the country. What you and your crew are building in these times is monumental, and I am so grateful for the leadership you are bringing.

"Let's Get Free": An Interview with Kate Shapiro of Southerners on New Ground (SONG)

For over two decades Southerners on New Ground (SONG) has been building up a multiracial base of member-leaders who are experimenting with focused campaigns to win reforms within a larger liberatory vision to shift culture and transform systems of oppression to systems of liberation. SONG is beautifully and powerfully Pro-Black, Pro-Working Class, Pro-Feminist, and Pro-Immigrant, and they are on the move in these Black Lives Matter times throughout the South.

From the beginning, SONG has been experimenting with ways of bringing more and more white LGBTQ people into liberation movements with racial justice at the center. They have a strategy of recruiting and developing white membership that can both support leadership from people of color in the organization and in communities of color, while also bringing leadership in white communities.

The national outrage of Black churches burning and the Charleston massacre—where a young white supremacist assassinated women, men, and young people gathered for a prayer meeting—and the national outcry against the Confederate flag growing has brought attention on the South. While many in the North and the West look

SONG members protest for BLM in Charleston, SC. Photo: Kate Shapiro

down on the South as the place where "racism really exists," it is critical that we remember that the flag of the slave society was and is the stars and stripes, that the entire political economy of the U.S. is built off of the stolen labor and systematic violence and evil of slavery, and that institutional racism is ingrained from sea to shining sea.

Furthermore, the South has a long history of leading many of the most dynamic, effective multiracial racial justice struggles in the country, from the days of slavery to today, which includes a long tradition of white anti-racist freedom fighters from leading abolitionist orators Angelina and Sarah Grimké of South Carolina to Civil Rights organizers Virginia Durr and Robert Graetz of Alabama, and Anne and Carl Braden of Kentucky, to the white anti-racist leaders Pam McMichael, Suzanne Pharr, and Mab Segrest of SONG in its 1992 founding, through today with leaders such as Caitlin Breedlove and Kate Shapiro.

We turn now to this interview with Kate Shapiro about the experiences, insights, and lessons from SONG's work to help inspire, equip, and support other white people around the country hungry for courageous action against white supremacy in these Black Lives Matter movement times and beyond. Let's get free.

Chris Crass: How are you working to move white people into the racial justice movement in this time? What's working? And what are you learning from what works?

Kate Shapiro: I am thrilled to have the opportunity to share some of our reflections from SONG's work over the last 22 years.

Southerners on New Ground (SONG) was founded after the 1992 LGBTQ Creating Change conference. Three Black lesbians and three white lesbians—Pat Hussain, Joan Garner, Mandy Carter, along with Suzanne Pharr, Pam McMichael, and Mab Segrest—are all organizers who had been working in the South. They saw the widening divide between white LGBTQ people and LGBTQ people of color and the issues that were being talked about and prioritized. They realized that there was a real need in the region, and throughout the movement nationally, to broaden and connect struggles for racial, economic, and gender justice that combat the right wing strategy of dividing us (as LGBTQ people) from each other along the fault lines of race, class, and culture. So, they started SONG and we have been working to answer the question of how to advance a multiracial, racial justice agenda over the entire lifespan of our organization.

"At SONG, rather than allyship, we think about building kinship."

SONG is currently putting our two decades of base building, deep relationship building, political analysis, and campaign support efforts to work through the initiation of Free From Fear campaigns. Free From Fear campaigns are local anti-criminalization campaigns anchored by SONG that address some of the key bleeding points in our community (LGBTQ and gender nonconforming, Black, or immigrant). We are advancing policy reforms by strengthening community police review boards, introducing anti-profiling ordinances, and pushing municipal court reforms around fines and fee structures while also maintaining our culture change work. Our campaign work is connected across the South and is targeted at local municipalities, rather than statewide fights.

SONG is made up of multiracial crews of members and staff in our Free From Fear sites. Currently those sites are Atlanta, Durham, and Richmond. More sites are emerging. These crews lead the hard and powerful work to vision, research, and launch the campaigns, as well as identify the different roles leaders can play in regards to identity and race. We welcome into this process our white members who want to learn campaign work, take risks, trust Black and immigrant and feminist leadership, be creative, be humble, be consistent, and really grow and do some work in the streets.

One of the things that this moment asks of us white people is to cash in our cultural and political capital that has been granted to us as white people through racism and to use it in the service of the work, of the collective. The goal is to move beyond a conversation about white privilege that can be really inhibiting. This means a lot of different things depending on the campaign and site (and this is something we are actively developing in real time). For some, it looks like positioning ourselves as white people inside progressive white organizations or our white churches. It means cashing in on some of our academic, political, and professional networks, using someone in our family, our lawyers, or political connections to bail our Black leaders out of jail.

At SONG, rather than allyship, we think about building kinship. That is a completely different orientation for us, and one that I have found to be much more potent. We need each other. We can't be whole by ourselves. Let's struggle and work to win. One of SONG's core beliefs is that there is no liberation, not even survival, in isolation. Our liberation depends on us coming together across lines of difference.

We know that now more than ever what this time calls for are deeply supported, trained up, and visionary LGBTQ people of color organizers. This is the primary focus of SONG's work. What is our role in making that happen? Part of that work is getting out of the way and getting up with our own white kin to take on white supremacy. Another part is inviting white LGBTQ people to join an organization that is advancing a strategy that centers on Black liberation and racial justice.

Chris: How do you think about effectiveness and how do you measure it? Can you share an experience that helps you think about effective work in white communities for racial justice?

Kate: We think about effectiveness in working with white leaders and in white communities in terms of leadership qualities we work to cultivate with our members. Our organizing approach is to combat our racist training and upbringing through our organizing campaigns and cultural work. Whether you are a white SONG member doing a LGBTQ film screening in Fayetteville, Arkansas, or tweeting at Ann Coulter, or introducing a citywide anti-profiling ordinance in your town, these are some of the expectations we have for each other in our work:

- Tenacity and sturdiness

- Humility

- Not overthinking and analyzing

- Expecting discomfort

- Willingness to try new things and struggle

- A desire to confront systemic power head on

- Imagination and creativity

- Ability/willingness to learn to build across class, race, and gender

- An understanding that trust is built and earned through time and work

Some other elements of leadership or effectiveness include:

- Full skill and resource transfer from white people to our Black and immigrant comrades (to combat hoarding and power over)

- Strong consistent flanking of our Black and immigrant comrades, which looks like everything from being co-conspirators, playing key roles in demonstrations and actions (training on direct action, media/communications, security, to being police liaison while people of color execute the action)

- Playing strategic roles within our coordinated campaign or culture change objectives with leadership of color

When I say role of white people I just want to be clear that SONG's context is particular, because we are primarily thinking about and throwing down with white LGBTQ people from, or living in, the South.

Chris: What are the goals and strategies (as emergent, planned, messy, and sophisticated, basic as they may be) you're operating from?

Kate: We have learned so much from the brilliance, courage, and vision of the leadership and work of Black Lives Matter and the Not1More Deportation Campaign. When I say we, I mean the leadership of our organization, both staff and members. Direct action plays such a critical role in these movement times. In large part, that is because they are not just random individual actions, but they function as a way to forward campaign goals or unite under a common vision. We know there is no substitute for those who are directly experiencing oppression to be on the front lines of civil disobedience. There is no substitution for undocumented people chaining themselves to the Southeast Regional office of ICE or having an all-Black shut down like the highway shutdown in Atlanta. White people have a role in supporting and advancing these goals. These lessons and approaches are woven into all of our work.

With our Free From Fear campaign work, we are building a regional strategy that compliments Free From Fear called Top 5 Enemies of the Queer South. What we are in the process of developing is how to take on key right wing institutions that benefit from the suffering of our people and contribute to the caging of our communities. This is going to be a place where our whole base, not just our white members, can take on one of these targets: from conversion therapy centers to right wing religious institutions. I personally feel really excited about going IN on some of these institutions with our white comrades.

Banner Hang in St. Louis, MO.
Photo: Jenny Truax

Similarly, we have white members in six different towns now organizing right wing radio call-ins (White Silence in the South Still Equals Death: Right Wing Radio Call-In Toolkit available at http://southernersonnewground.org/radiotoolkit/) as a political intervention after the Emanuel AME Massacre in Charleston. After the massacre, we saw the media erroneously spin the attack as a gun control debate and the assailant as a "lone wolf." So we are challenging ourselves and other white people to engage these pundits in a conversation, not to persuade them to join the Homosexual Revolution, but to challenge their hegemony and the power they have over the airways. This work is about building our collective muscle to fight and share a different story, vision, and understanding, especially with the other white people who may be listening to these shows. I also share this because it's an example of what we mean by experimentation—Will we get on the radio? How will the pundits react when we do? This intervention allows us to step into the rink and to try to figure out how to directly access some of our cultural war opponents, who are creating and reinforcing so much hatred and consequent violence. Some of our members in Atlanta got on the radio the other day and were so pumped after listening to right wing radio for five days and stressing all the way out.

Chris: What challenges are you facing? How are you trying to overcome them? What are you learning from these experiences?

Kate: This past year, Caitlin Breedlove and I, as white people working in leadership in SONG, wrote a tool called "There Is Honor in The Work: SONG on the Role of White People in The Movement at This Time" (http://southernersonnewground.org/2015/03/white-people-movement-role/). In the tool, we lay out a kind of laundry list of challenges we think we need to confront in order to build a stronger multiracial movement. Lots of the challenges we face are about leadership characteristics and conduct. We see conduct, how we are/act/show up, to be a real barrier to building authentic relationships and work across class, race, and gender. People of color are already demonstrating a LOT of generosity to be even messing with some of us white people. We didn't build the tool for ourselves or others to get stuck in the individual/interpersonal dynamics as so many of us have been taught to do, but instead to say that we can't take on institutional racism while working alongside people of color if we don't know how to act. It's just going to flop.

SONG is an organization that is not neutral about race, leadership, and conduct. We are Pro-Black, Pro-Working Class, Pro-Feminist, and Pro-Immigrant, and that freaks people out. We are loud, scrappy, boisterous, raunchy, hard-working, deeply devoted, blunt, and direct. The people we're looking for are the ones that come back and who aren't afraid to overcome their personal challenges in the name of the work.

One of the challenges with some of our white family is hesitancy. We see white people get in their brains and drop out or pull back because they want to be useful but they're not getting a certain level of hand holding. To that end, SONG has a six-page leadership agreement document that all of our member-leaders and sites SIGN onto that is all about conduct. It gives us a way to rebuild our covenant with each other and build in accountability as we grow the organization.

> **"...demonstrate your commitment to local Black leadership through simple and humble acts."**

While the majority of U.S. cities with the highest segregation are not in the South, we know that segregation and deliberate separation of white communities from black communities because of fear and loathing of Black people is very, very real here as well. So one of the things I have encouraged our different members to do, to get out of their heads and develop their practice, especially those who haven't ever been in real relationship with Black communities or people, is to volunteer at a local Black-led organization. Sweep the floors, stuff envelopes, do whatever needs to be done, set up for meetings, etc. If you have resources, commit or donate them without controlling the work or telling people how they should be doing their work. Commit for a year and demonstrate your commitment to local Black leadership through simple and humble acts. I remember when I first moved back to Atlanta in 2006 and I just showed up over and over at the Hunger Coalition (statewide, very, very grassroots, Black-led, anti-hunger and anti-poverty organization) to do what needed to be done. They were understandably wary and welcoming of this chipper young white girl and slowly, through action, that trust was built. Now they are deep political family and one of our closest local partners.

Another challenge is, while in the campaign sites, we get shade from other white people who say that our work is reformist rather than radical. They say things like, "…but the police will still exist even if you change their right to profile and harass people…". We often get this from people who became political through academia and are used to a certain type of critique. This has been a challenge especially as some of our member-leaders are new to organizing work and unrelenting critique early on is pretty bad for morale. It's been important to go back to what it means to honor, trust, and align with the leadership of people of color, especially Black women in our case with the Free From Fear work. It's important to know how to maintain steadfastness and build trust even when you're getting shade from your friends. We know we need liberatory vision in our organizing work that imagines a different world, and we need campaigns that address the day-to-day violence that our people experience. We need them when, as SONG organizer Mary Hooks says, "the boot is on our neck." As white people we have a duty and responsibility to move with this urgency and not get stuck in a lifelong processing session about theory.

> **"…we need liberatory vision in our organizing work that imagines a different world…"**

For a lot of our rural and smaller-town white membership, SONG spaces, especially regional gatherings, are when they are around the most LGBTQ people they will be around all year, and very often the most LGBTQ people of color they will be around all year. This brings up a lot for folks! Two dynamics often play out: some white people decide to only build with other white people because they are scared of people of color, while some white people turn their backs on other white people because they only want to align themselves with people of color. The way we address this is by setting up accountability buddies amongst and between white people who are moving and working together. This is a way to build relationships and instill a formalized sense of co-development.

Chris: How are you developing your own leadership and the leadership of people around you to step up in these profound, painful, and powerful Black Lives Matter movement times?

Kate: On a personal and organizational level, we draw great strength, inspiration, and power from Black Lives Matter. How do we align around Black Lives Matter? This is a question for all sections of our base: white, Black, immigrant, rural LGBTQ Southerners, all of us. Each part of our base has its own answers, so as an organization our response has to be multi-pronged and strategic to support and follow the work, direction, and action of our Black leadership.

My comrade Mary Hooks represents SONG on the National Planning Committee for Black Lives Matter. SONG is working to build a Black Lives Matter Cohort of our folks who are throwing down in our Free From Fear campaigns. This cohort will support and train up a crew of Black LGBTQ leaders in SONG and the region who are networked together, know how to run campaigns from beginning to end, and are uplinked into this fantastic, visionary, disciplined national Black Lives Matter crew.

Black Lives Matter gives white people the opportunity to align ourselves in action with Black communities. It gives us the opportunity to act out some of the things I was talking about above—getting out of the way, making key interventions with other white people, and leveraging our skills and knowledge to support Black leadership. For example, we have a crew of member-leaders in Charleston, South Carolina, who led a civil disobedience the month after Walter Scott was murdered and led a profoundly beautiful March for Black Lives on the Saturday after the AME Massacre. They aimed to create a space for public grief, rage, and uplift—and they achieved that on all counts. Two days after, our white crew led an action in downtown Charleston that explicitly spoke to our responsibility to confront racism and to contest the white-led "all lives matter" narrative that had taken root in Charleston.

Jillian Brandl, a white SONG member-leader in Charleston, said part of the role of white folks in this time is to handle our emotions in a way that does not overshadow and silence the experience of people of color. Our role is to uplift and amplify people of color leadership despite our discomfort or our fear.

Another important question we must ask and answer is: "What is the role of white people in anticipating and intervening on backlash to Black-led organizing?" Five Southern Black churches were burned in the two weeks following the AME Massacre. How do we respond to that? Jennicet Eva Gutiérrez, the wildly courageous undocumented transwoman leader who interrupted Obama's speech to demand an end to trans detention, was shouted down by white gay and lesbian people in the room. How do we respond to that? These are our problems as white people to not just grapple with but to intervene on.

The question of our lifetime is, Which side are you on? What I know now more than ever is that it matters so much more what we DO, not what we say or think. Black Lives Matter reminds me of this every day. Let's be brave, courageous, and loving and do the damn thing.

....

Kate Shapiro *is the membership director of Southerners on New Ground, the largest grassroots multiracial LGBTQ organization in the South. She has devoted the majority of her days to community organizing for the last 10 years; her people are a fascinating combination of scrappy New York Jews and WASPY West Virginia timber barons (and defiant, loving, and raucous liberation-minded LGBTQIA people). She wants to thank SONG member leaders Jade Brooks, Jillian Brandl, and Micah Blaise for feedback and thoughts for this interview.*

To learn more about Southerners on New Ground, go to
www.southernersonnewground.org.

How "All Lives Matter" Is Vandalizing Our Theology and Values

Someone vandalized a Black Lives Matter banner, crossing out "Black" and writing "All" at the First Jefferson Unitarian Universalist Church of Fort Worth, Texas. Yes, this is outrageous, and it must be said that every Unitarian Universalist or other progressive person of faith who argues for "All" rather than "Black" is also committing an act of vandalism. They are vandalizing our theological commitments to racial justice and our spiritual values of Beloved Community. Because, let's be clear, if you still think "All" after Black Lives Matter is explained, then, like the vandalism, it isn't about inclusion of "everyone," it's about eliminating "Black" in a fiercely anti-Black racist society and re-centering white people's need to feel, well, at the center of everything.

Love to my beautiful Unitarian Universalist family in Fort Worth who put out a powerful statement on why they stand in solidarity for Black Lives Matter and have committed to replacing their banner, no matter how many times it is vandalized. Love to the hundreds of Unitarian Universalist churches who have also placed banners in highly visible places in front of their churches. As white people of faith, we don't just act in solidarity; we also act to save all of our souls from the monstrosity of white supremacy.

Clergy March in Ferguson, MO. Photo: Margaret Ernst

For Activists Devastated and Feeling Defeated by Racist Violence

1. Take a moment to appreciate the fact that you are devastated by brutal racist injustice and that, while your heart is broken, a much worse alternative would be that your heart was hardened by the scarring of internalizing white supremacy that divested you from loving your own full humanity and the humanity of others.

Your devastation is the result of your heart being alive and refusing the socialized indifference, amnesia, and straight-jacketing of your consciousness that post-Civil Rights movement white supremacy aims for. Your internal capacity to be devastated by this murderous racist system is a source of power that serves you well and is what can help you be part of bringing this system down.

2. Focus your attention on momentum for justice, and decentralize the roadblocks and jackasses. At this moment, there are millions of people in motion for Black liberation. Courageous Black feminist leadership is front and center. The vision, strategy, inspiration, and guidance of the leaderful Black Lives Matter movement is where our attention should be. Not on the right wing jackasses, militant post-racial racist trolls, people in your life who just want to argue, or other energy-sucking dementors that grab and hold our attention. They too often make it hard to see the people around us in motion, or those ready to move, for racial justice.

Ask yourself some questions. Am I letting jackasses who want to maintain supremacy systems occupy my heart and mind? (We are socialized to do this, socialized to undermine our efforts to get free.) Or, are we choosing to open our hearts and minds to the leaders who give us energy, who give us hope, who connect us to ancestral liberation movements and movements of liberation and humanity loving people today?

3. Be loving with yourself. Supremacy systems want you to exhaust yourself by beating yourself up—for not doing enough, for letting jackasses demobilize you, for "not being good enough" to be the activist you want to be. Tell these voices of supremacy systems that they cannot have you, that you are stronger than they would ever allow you to believe, and that our movement is far stronger, and more effective, than supremacy systems want us to understand, to feel in our bones, to feel as tears of pain and sorrow roll down our faces.

4. Take time to learn about grassroots Black Lives Matter organizing, led by Black activists, but also about what activists racialized as white are doing as well. Try to

know three inspiring, life-affirming stories of resistance for each story of devastating racist violence. One of the key challenges before us isn't just awakening white racialized people to the reality of racism, but to help ourselves and others truly believe we can bring it down and build up robust, complex, living and breathing Beloved Community. We are carrying on the legacies of our movement ancestors and the impact of our efforts is beyond what we often dare allow ourselves to dream.

Rally for BLM at State Capitol in Austin, TX. Photo: Hannah Williams

"Let courageous liberation leadership move you..."

5. For every Ida B. Wells, Anne Braden, William Lloyd Garrison, W.E.B. Du Bois, Ella Baker, Elizabeth "Betita" Martinez, and Alicia Garza, there are millions of people whose names we don't know. They threw down and are throwing down, in many different ways. They give what they can with talents, capacities, and other responsibilities they have. United by vision, strategy, culture, love, and rage; this is what makes movements happen.

What you do matters.

You are not alone.

Let courageous liberation leadership move you, and protect yourself from the forces that seek to demobilize, defeat, and undermine you and forces for collective liberation.

6. Reach out to others, as you are, and generate mutual support, as many are having or have had these same struggles. Refuse the isolation supremacy systems seek for you. Accept the interdependence liberation calls us into, even when supremacy systems tell us we aren't good enough to experience it. Love is on our side. We will get free, all of us.

Throwing Down Against White Supremacy Is Sacred Work: An Interview with Rev. Anne D. Dunlap of United Church of Christ

As white activists around the country, including faith-based activists of nearly every denomination, work to step up in these Black Lives Matter movement times, Rev. Anne D. Dunlap provides us all with pastoral care and spiritually rooted vision. In this interview, Rev. Dunlap shares lessons and insights from her anti-racist work in white communities, her multiracial alliance building efforts, and her liberation theology. Let her reflections help embolden and nourish us, as we build, together, for collective liberation, with Black Lives Matter at the core. This is sacred work.

Chris Crass: How are you working to move white people into the racial justice movement in this time? What's working? And what are you learning from what works?

Rev. Anne Dunlap: I have been a faith-rooted justice movement activist and leader for a long time (nearly 30 years if you go back to my "call" into the work at age sixteen that launched this trajectory of my life) in many capacities, and most often as a "bridge" between white folk/communities and marginalized folk/communities. Whether it's racial and economic justice, police brutality, detention abolition, deportation resistance, or indigenous rights, I do pastoral solidarity work as well as constantly trying to get more white folk involved. I'm also a leader with our local SURJ (Showing Up for Racial Justice) chapter and I'm doing some work with SURJ nationally to engage white faith communities in being bolder for racial justice. More in-

formally, I have lots of conversations with white friends and colleagues about how we can show up, and how we show up, in the work for racial justice. Resource sharing is incredibly important here, whether by social media or sending a friend my favorite Andrea Smith resource.

One thing I have noticed is that, as a white clergyperson who shows up often in pretty public ways, I am finding white people seek me out for conversations to talk through how they might do that too, or that they

BLM Rally in Denver, CO.
Photo: Rev. Brandee Jasmine Mimitzraiem

find themselves emboldened to take action where they are because they have seen me do it. I take that to mean that white folk are longing for some white models for

153

racial justice and solidarity, and so we need those of us more practiced at it and/or are willing to "be public" to continue to do that, and encourage more folks to try it. And here I don't mean posting your selfie at the latest action, but more importantly being public about our questions and wrestlings, being public about our mistakes, being public about the resources we find helpful, being public about our horror at what is continuing to be done in our name. If I might channel my mentor, Dr. Vincent Harding, let people see you be fully human in this messy, magnificent work that is the freedom movement.

> **"I take that to mean that white folk are longing for some white models for racial justice and solidarity, and so we need those of us more practiced at it and/or are willing to "be public" to continue to do that, and encourage more folks to try it."**

To that I would add a couple of things: (1) recognizing that I am not an expert or THE model and being clear that although I have been at this a long time, I am also always just beginning; and (2) being public does not mean centering myself as a white person and thus de-centering the voices, experiences, and lives of Black, Latina/o, indigenous, immigrant, etc., folk. That can be a tricky dance, to both not hide and also not center my white self, and I am sure I don't always get it right.

Chris: How do you think about effectiveness and how do you measure it? Can you share an experience that helps you think about effective work in white communities for racial justice?

Anne: As a spiritual leader rooted in radical Christian tradition and informed by liberationist, feminist/womanist, and post-colonial praxis, I have to ask: How do we understand "effectiveness" in ways that are non-capitalist? Capitalism is its own theological system that I find runs completely counter to what my tradition teaches. Capitalist "effectiveness" is driven by numbers, by production as if humans were cogs in machine, by increasing profit and consumption, and by continuous extraction of resources regardless of impact, dividing up "winners" (most worthy) "and losers."

Capitalist "effectiveness" requires, as Andrea Smith writes, perpetual enslavement of Black bodies, perpetual disappearance of indigenous bodies, perpetual war against the "foreign threat" of brown bodies. I'm not interested in those definitions of effectiveness.

What is "effectiveness" that is prophetic and revolutionary, that honors the wholeness of human dignity and the tender fragility of human lives and bodies, that honors not only human life but all creatures—flora, fauna, mineral, liquid, vapor? One experience that helps me think about this is an action I participated in 2007, a nonviolent act of resistance against the Columbus Day parade in Denver that resulted in nearly a hundred of us being arrested and being pretty brutalized by the Denver police, both in the street and in the jail. I helped organize students, faculty, and staff at the Iliff School of Theology where I was a student leader at the time, and we had a group of 11 students and alums who were among those arrested, and nearly forty more present.

Rev. Dunlap speaking at BLM rally. Photo: American Friends Service Committee, Denver

From the capitalist view one might argue this action was not "effective." We were arrested, the parade was continued, and almost all of us who went to trial were found guilty of violating the city's "parade ordinance" (put in place to prevent protests of the Columbus Day parade), resisting arrest, and other charges. The Denver police were never held accountable for their brutality against us. Some of us continue to live with the trauma to our bodies and psyches from that day. The whole event and its aftermath of trials and healing took immense resources and energy. Was this an effective action?

To answer from what I might call the prophetic view, this is what I see: white students at Iliff emboldened to take action on this and other justice issues, including white parents who went to their children's schools to get curriculum about Columbus changed; healers who stepped up and identified themselves and have continued to provide for the community's healing; relationships of solidarity, trust, and fierce love that were born that day and continue; and, for many white folk including myself, the breaking apart of the veil of "legitimacy" of the "justice system" and policing, and how both of those systems actually serve to perpetuate white supremacy. I am still seeing the impact of that action to this day in our community; the city thought they had won, but the result was a stronger multiracial community of resistance in Denver, and with white folks pretty radicalized by our experience (whether as arrestees, witnesses, or seeing the aftermath).

This is the kind of effectiveness our tradition teaches us is possible: turning the wisdom of the world on its head, what the Roman Empire determined as "effective"—executing the radical Jesus by crucifixion—was rendered as foolishness when the Spirit-filled community rose up in resistance with their ringing proclamation that the Empire had no power over life or death: "Christ is risen!"

Chris: What are the goals and strategies (as emergent, planned, messy, and sophisticated, basic as they may be) you're operating from?

Anne: My big goal—and I believe this is the "big goal" the Divine attests to and longs for us in our tradition—is the total undoing of white supremacist capitalist heteropatriarchy (again, Andrea Smith) for a world in which all life, not only human but creatures and the land as well, can flourish. To get there my part is to be in deep human relationship with marginalized communities, and to work with white folk and faith communities in particular.

We need as many nimble tools as possible for collective liberation. Besides the organizing work and just plain showing up for actions and such, some other tools include:

For white folk who claim to be Christian: recovering and immersing ourselves in the liberative and revolutionary sources, biblical and theological, of Christian tradition, and sharing and embodying those. This includes perpetually reminding ourselves that the Bible is not the victory handbook of the Empire, but the outcry and deeply human wrestlings of the oppressed.

Educating ourselves all the time, especially through listening to oppressed voices. And letting those voices interrogate us deeply, letting them make us confront the ways white supremacy lives inside our heads. This is the unsexy (because often invisible) work of disrupting whiteness as a white person and just as important as showing up publically, because it helps us know how to show up in better, more liberative ways.

Learning the "people's history" of struggle and liberation, including the local history of where we live, and sharing it.

Knowing our limits and doing our own healing work. This is so important and must not be overlooked. Therapy, herbal practice, Sabbath, physical labor at my friend's goat farm, and spiritual direction all help keep me going and help me bring my best, most-grounded self to the work, and I publically encourage and affirm other folks' efforts towards self-care.

A word about spiritual direction: I find this helps me cultivate discernment, holds space for my vocational wrestlings in the face of challenge, and fosters my ability to sit in the unknown and trust there is more going on here than I am aware of; this last in particular allows me to let go of the control that is one way whiteness perpetuates itself.

Chris: What challenges are you facing? How are you trying to overcome them? What are you learning from these experiences?

> **"I've learned to remind myself that I am not the center of the movement, and a healthy me, even if I'm not at everything, is so much better for the movement than a burned-out me."**

Anne: There are a couple of main ones for me.

1. Institutions. Entrenched oppressions in institutions, including and especially the church and the academy, and the institutional capacity for self-preservation rather than liberation challenge me at the deepest level and cause me the most despair! Community, both close friends and a community of solidarity, is so much help in navigating this challenge. I have also learned that if there is no space for movement, no space for Spirit to crack something open, it might be best to walk away, and I have done that on occasion—not walk away from the freedom movement, but from that particular institution that will take my life in ways I am not willing to give it up. Everyone must do their own discernment around this; I may leave where another person may stay, and that's cool

2. Being Overwhelmed. Constantly confronting injustice and the death-dealing powers of Empire is wearying enough, and I think our saturation with 24-hour news cycles and constant social media updates can sometimes make this worse (though social media is great for connecting and expressing solidarity). I have to be sure to take Sabbath time to rest, integrate, tend to my spirit and body and home. As a white person I have struggled with this because the temptation to be the "perfect ally" who shows up to everything is very strong (and capitalist-driven); I've learned to remind myself that I am not the center of the movement, and a healthy me, even if I'm not at everything, is so much better for the movement than a burned-out me.

Chris: How are you developing your own leadership and the leadership of people around you to step up in these profound, painful, and powerful Black Lives Matter movement times?

Anne: As I mentioned, I have been in this work a long time, though focused more on immigration and economic justice. Last year two things happened that prompted some deep vocational discernment for me: Dr. Vincent Harding died, a loss I grieved deeply, and a few months later Michael Brown was killed. These are connected for me because Michael Brown was killed not long after Dr. Harding's memorial service here in Denver, and I began to talk to Dr. Harding every day, asking him what I should do. It soon became clear that I was being called to deepen my justice work through the Black Lives Matter movement, and to do so by leaving my prior congregational position and embracing my role as "street pastor" as well as responding to the outcry for white folks to educate white folks—in part, by getting involved in SURJ.

In these intervening months I have utilized this "in-between" time of unknown in terms of a particular job by reading everything I can, taking advantage of trainings, finding resources for working on collective liberation with white folks and white church folks, trying on some new ways of reclaiming my voice as a leader, and most importantly building relationships and showing up in solidarity with our Black Lives Matter leaders in Denver. In a sense, I feel like these last eight months in many ways have been a preparation for some amazing and difficult work that is about to unfold.

....

Rev. Anne Dunlap *is an ordained United Church of Christ minister serving as a "street pastor" for racial justice and solidarity in the Denver, Colorado, area. Rev. Dunlap is committed to the work of justice and liberation, working in freedom movements with folks across race, gender, and class lines for over 25 years—with a particular passion for solidarity with black, immigrant, worker, and indigenous communities. She was named Outstanding Alumna in 2011 from the Iliff School of Theology, where she also serves as adjunct faculty. In addition Anne is working with SURJ (Showing Up for Racial Justice) to organize white faith communities for racial justice work, and is a contributor at the UCC's New Sacred blog.*

To read the UCC's New Sacred blog, go to www.newsacred.org.

We Must Weather the Storm to See the Rainbow:
An Open Love Letter to White Unitarian Universalists (and Other White People Too) Struggling with Their Commitment to Black Lives Matter

Our commitment to living the values of our faith is being tested. We are standing in the storm of reaction against the Black Lives Matter movement. Now is the time when we must ask ourselves, "Do we become even more out and proud for racial justice, or do we shrink down in retreat?"

With FOX news leading a media frenzy denouncing the Black Lives Matter movement as a hate group, as terrorists, as anti-white, some of us are retreating from wearing Black Lives Matter buttons and some of us are questioning whether or not to take down the Black Lives Matter banners from our churches.

It would be easy for me to say that all of the white UUs who are faltering are just falling back into their white privilege, are sinking back into their liberal white racism. It would be easy for me to distance myself and feel superior. It is much harder for me to say that I too, as a white Unitarian Universalist, have been scared. After months of wearing my Black Lives Matter button, I found myself second-guessing whether to wear it.

What if I am challenged at the grocery store or walking in the park with my son. It was much easier to wear my button after the latest police murder of an unarmed Black person. Filled with anger and a desire to "do something," I wore my button with defiance to racism and a commitment to racial justice.

I held my button in my hand, and I knew that all of this is much bigger than buttons and banners. This is about breaking a centuries-old code of white silence and white consent for anti-Black racist violence and institutional white supremacy and its legal and cultural dispersal of white privilege and white entitlement. Entitlement to safety and comfort, at the expense of people of color having the same. Entitlement to our children not needing to think about the color of their skin or wondering if the color of their skin puts them at risk of socially and state-sanctioned violence.

This is about choosing what side of justice we put our bodies on. And, like other white UUs, I don't want to be part of this racist society. I want to stand in the tradition of Unitarian Universalist abolitionists and Civil Rights workers, knowing that even within our faith tradition it has not always been easy. I want to stand on the side of love, like we did on Marriage Equality, even when it was illegal in every state and scary for many of us to be publically out for LGBTQ rights.

The Black Lives Matter movement is the leading struggle for racial justice of our times. It is a movement led by Black people who are women, queer, youth, working class, including Black UUs around the country. It is a movement to end institutional racism and to respect the inherent worth and dignity of all people. It is a movement for collective liberation. And it is a movement that puts a challenge to every white person who believes themselves a proponent of racial equality, every white person inspired by the Civil Rights movement, every white person who believes they would be on the right side of history if an injustice of great magnitude were taking place.

Weekly Vigil in Chesterfield, MO led by Emerson Unitarian Universalist Church.
Photo: Nora Rasman

The movement is challenging us to put our values into practice— not just when it is easy, but also when it is hard. It is the challenge to be honest with ourselves and admit that people who espouse "All Lives Matter," even in our congregations, aren't always confused; in fact, often they are quite clear.

The All Lives Matter reaction, just like the white people who decried Civil Rights as "special rights" in the 1960s, is based in white resentment and anger towards assertions of Black equality and Black humanity, particularly when those assertions disrupt the "normal (racially unequal) order."

We are living in Black Lives Matter times. Times when a movement of everyday people with Black people in the lead is on-the-move, opposing injustices of a great magnitude. To help me have courage in these times, I have created a ritual out of putting on my Black Lives Matter button, and I invite you to create one for yourself, as well. I put on my Black Lives Matter button as a ritual of rededicating myself to daily action for racial justice. I hold my button between my hands and pray. I pray for the movement to continue growing more and more powerful. I pray that more and more white people awaken from the nightmare of white supremacy and join the fight for the dream of beloved community.

I pray and call forward the names of ancestors—from Harriet Tubman and William Lloyd Garrison to Ella Baker and Anne Braden. I pray for the leadership of Alicia Garza, Patrisse Cullors, Opal Tometi, Elandria Williams, Carla Wallace, Tufara Muhammad, Meredith Martin-Moates, Rev. Osagyefo Sekou, Rev. Ashley Horan, Leslie Mac, Ash-Lee Henderson, and the many others who are building this deeply life-affirming movement, everyday.

I pray that the racist nightmare against communities of color ends. I reflect on the moments I'm scared wearing this button, recognize how miniscule it is, and meditate on the daily devastation of anti-Black racism on the lives of Black people in my life and in society. And then I pray for my four-year-old son, River, and his little one month-old brother, August. I remember how, when I grew up, the most vocal people in the white community speaking about race were racists. I pray that my sons grow up with courageous, passionate, visionary, white anti-racist leaders in every part of this society.

I pray that white UUs, in the hundreds of thousands, act in the tradition of white UU Civil Rights martyrs Viola Liuzzo and James Reeb, and not join in the All Lives Matter reaction and act from the tradition of white racism that killed them.

I rededicate myself to actively supporting UU congregations and members around the country who are standing on the side of Black Lives Matter through banners, weekly vigils, fundraising for Black-led racial justice organizing in their community, inviting Black Lives Matter leaders to preach at their pulpits, writing op-eds for the local newspapers, holding press conferences when their banners are vandalized, and bringing their spiritual and religious leadership into the streets for marches and civil disobedience.

River Road UU Church of Maryland in Selma, AL for 50th Anniversary. Photo: Chris Crass

I spoke with a UU minister of a majority white congregation who has had their Black Lives Matter banner vandalized multiple times and who have been in the national press as a result. Tears filled my eyes as I listened to her talk about how the congregation is struggling through fear of feeling under attack, confronting their white privilege, and, despite the racist backlash, staying true to their values. We talked about this being the moment for her congregation, and white UUs throughout our denomination, to either open their hearts more fully and act with courage, or move back into white silence, white consent, and white privilege. These are the times that our church was intended for, to help us act with courage in the face of fear and hate.

These are the times for us to use our spiritual traditions and rituals and act as a faith, to join the leading movement for racial justice of our time and weather the storm together. We must weather the storm, so we can experience the rainbow of collective liberation. And, around our faith today, there are tens of thousands of UUs—Black UUs, UUs of color, white UUs—who are on-the-move for Black Lives Matter. Our church is in the streets and our faith calls us into prophetic action. This is our mission in practice.

We can do this! And to help, here are five suggestions for those of us who are working through fear and uncertainty to make a commitment to Black Lives Matter, and then ten suggestions for those who have been committed and want to step up their involvement in the movement.

For those of us just getting started:

1. Just as you would tell a friend and someone in your family to stop listening to FOX news and the corporate media about the realities of climate change, stop listening to them about what the Black Lives Matter movement is really about. Look for essays and interviews with Alicia Garza, Patrisse Cullors, Cornel West, and Rev. Osagyefo Sekou.

2. Reach out to another white person in your congregation who is involved in Black Lives Matter and racial justice issues. Ask if there is a time when you could get together to hear more about their own journey with this work and ask for support.

3. Reach out to your minister or lay leaders in the congregation for pastoral care as you work through what is holding you back.

4. Look for opportunities at church for discussion groups, film nights, or a group of people to go to the next Black Lives Matter rally with.

5. Pray, sing, meditate, go for a walk somewhere beautiful, and take time to draw inspiration from the sacred and gather your courage and fortitude to work against the death culture of white supremacy, knowing that this is the path towards beloved community.

For those of us who want to step up our work for Black Lives Matter:

1. Start wearing Black Lives Matter buttons and t-shirts, and get extras to share with friends, family, and people in your congregation. Develop your own ritual of putting on the button as a commitment to taking daily acts for racial justice and Black liberation. Better yet, get a group of people together by your church to pitch in and order a few hundred buttons online.

Ask your minister if a special message can be given at a Sunday service about the ritual of the button and distribute them to the congregation. If there are enough, ask each member of the church to take an extra button to give to someone in their lives as an act of building the base of support for Black Lives Matter. You can order buttons from "Working Against Racism," which is a multiracial group of Black Lives Matter activists who, for reasons of geography or disability, cannot be part of a face-to-face group, and are focused on visibility efforts. You can contact workingagainstracism@gmail.com for ordering info and prices.

2. Hang a Black Lives Matter banner in front of your church as a tool for internal and external consciousness raising and as an act of concrete solidarity. Build a core of people who strongly support this and are prepared to speak on why this should be done. Recruit and build support with many people who have formal and informal influence/power in the church. Find out what process you need to go through to make this happen.

Ask other congregations who have hung banners for advice on how to successfully move forward in your congregation. Hold "lead up" discussions before the vote to raise awareness internally in the congregation. Then hang the banner to show solidarity externally, and embolden the congregation to live into what that statement calls for.

3. Prepare for the racist backlash to the banner by developing the anti-racist leadership of the congregation. As you know, many UU churches have had their Black Lives Matter banners vandalized or stolen, and many have received an outpouring of racist reaction and even threats for putting up the banner.

In your work building support for the banner, also build up the anti-racist resilience of the congregation to face this opposition with courage and to use the racist opposition as an opportunity to speak even more loudly in your community for racial justice. For example, many UU churches have held press conferences after their banners have been vandalized and have spoken powerfully about why they hung their banners, and what it means as religious communities to be on the side of love and Black Lives Matter.

Let our opposition create opportunities to deepen our work, and amplify our voices—but, to do so, we must support members of the congregation to speak in their own voices about why they are taking this stand. You can do this by role playing difficult conversations and sharing talking points during a special community discussion, and create opportunities for members of the congregation to share reflections from challenging moments in Sunday services.

Facing this racist opposition, by drawing on our theology and the power of our spiritual community, is an opportunity to collectively live our faith for justice.

4. Invite a Black leader in this new movement, from your local community or region, to give a sermon at the church and give the speaker an honorarium of between

$500–1000. Have church leaders promote this sermon and preach the week before about why this will be an important service for the community.

Use this as an opportunity to demonstrate public commitment of the congregation to Black Lives Matter, and also deepen the understanding of what the movement is about in the congregation. Also host white anti-racist leaders who are involved in Black Lives Matter. Invite white anti-racists who can help speak to the journey of becoming white anti-racists and provide concrete examples of white people taking action for racial justice.

5. Encourage congregation to show up and participate in local/regional marches, demonstrations, and vigils. Or, hold your own regular vigil, as many UU churches are doing. Ask the minister or others with sway in the church to speak in the services the week before the march/action on how this is a moment to practice your faith in public.

"...use gratitude and appreciation to open your heart to possibility and the beautiful connections we make in the-work of building a new way towards collective liberation."

Do a prep training on going to marches/actions to help support those who have never gone before. Go as a group, and pray/sing before and after as a way of helping create church in the streets. Our goal is to be powerful together for justice, to help build courage over fear, and to move our faith, effectively, into action for Black Lives Matter.

6. Encourage the congregation to reach out to local Black Lives Matter organizers and activists and offer the congregation as a free meeting and event space. This could also include the congregation providing food, childcare, and other support for those meetings and events—which also creates opportunities for people in the congregation to be involved who might not want to go to a march, but who want to show up in other ways. And it's a good way to build relationships between congregation and leaders/organizers in the Black Lives Matter movement 7. Hold fundraisers at the church for local, regional, and national Black Lives Matter movement efforts. Use this as an opportunity for members of the congregation to invite people

from their personal networks to come. This can be a way to raise money to support Black-led work, and build up the confidence of the congregation to speak to people beyond the church about why the movement for Black lives is so important. Fundraisers are also a way to build up beloved community united for racial justice.

8. Provide money and resources to support youth and young adult anti-racist/racial justice activists in your church to organize their networks for Black Lives Matter. Support the youth groups in your church to hold group discussions and go to marches and demonstrations together.

The youth and young adults in our churches are often in the lead on anti-racism and racial justice. Be sure to include their leadership in your efforts as well as bringing support to following their leadership in the efforts they are mobilizing. It is important for our denomination to remember and honor that it was the youth caucus at the 2015 General Assembly in Portland that led the effort to pass the Action of Immediate Witness in support of Black Lives Matter.

9. Get involved with your local chapter of the national white anti-racist network Showing Up for Racial Justice (SURJ). Go to http://www.showingupforracialjustice. org/ for outstanding white anti-racist organizing resources and to either find a local contact or download the toolkit on starting a local chapter. Unitarian Universalists have been involved in SURJ since the beginning, and many UU individuals and congregations are heavily involved around the country. This is a great way to get white racial justice activists in the church involved in organizing the broader white community with the goal of uniting white people to the multiracial movement for justice.

10. Love yourself and love the people around you dedicated to this work. Take moments to pause and express gratitude and appreciation to yourself for working through the challenges you have faced and build your internal power for the challenges ahead. Take moments to express love and gratitude to the people around you who inspire you, who keep you moving when it gets hard, who you see taking risks, who you are thankful to be in the world and in this work with.

White supremacy and systems of supremacy depend on us feeling hopeless and alienated. Develop spiritual rituals of defiance to this divide-and-rule strategy and use gratitude and appreciation to open your heart to possibility and the beautiful connections we make in the work of building a new way towards collective liberation.

"To Nourish and Sustain Us":
A Poem on the Third Anniversary of Trayvon Martin's Murder

To the mother who shared the story of her heart breaking when her six-year-old autistic son told her, "don't worry mom, they won't kill me, I'm white,"

To the mothers, fathers, and babas who have thanked me for speaking out as a white person, because they are so afraid that their Black children could be next,

To the mother of a family of biological and adopted children who explained that since the murder of Trayvon, her young white daughter has lived in fear of her twenty-year-old Black brother being killed, so scared that she had her Brother call every night to tell her he was ok,

To the white people, around the country, who have reached out hungry for direction on what we can do to challenge white supremacy, end the criminalization and violence against communities of color, and do the right thing,

To the organizers and activists of color who have expressed their anger, frustration, and disappointment that more white people aren't stepping up more often to take on racism and that, even in this moment of naked truth, too many are still making excuses to not look directly at it, or trying to reduce the power of this moment of historic and institutional racism making itself plain, reducing its meaning to just being about bad individuals,

To Alicia Garza for writing a love letter to the Black community on the night that George Zimmerman was acquitted, and in that love letter declaring #BlackLivesMatter. To Patrisse Cullors and Opal Tometi for joining with Alicia to co-found Black Lives Matter as an online and in-the-streets political project to remake the world. And to all the Black leaders, cultural organizers, new and longtime activists, family and friends who have lost loved ones at the hand of the state, who have thrown down to make Black Lives Matter a movement on-the-move,

To the white anti-racists, feminists, social justice activists—overwhelmingly women, queer, working class, genderqueer, transgender, Jewish, and fabulous—who are stepping up into the whirlwind of these times to bring clarity, leadership, vulnerability, analysis, and love,

To the white men, from all over the country, who have thanked me, often with a tear in their eye, for speaking about the nightmare of white supremacy and patriarchy in our lives, for calling other white men into action for collective liberation, and for believing in our ability to heal and rock it. To the two white teenage boys who told me they had never seen a white person speak passionately against racism before, and said that while they knew what kind of person they didn't want to become, until I talked about the tradition of white anti-racist activists, including men like William Lloyd Garrison, Carl Braden, David Gilbert, Scott Winn, and James Haslam, they didn't know they had role models to inspire who they could become,

To all of the beautiful people who, despite the viciousness of anti-Black racism in this country, who, despite seeing the racist structures of the United States exposed, who, despite all efforts to tell us that we are powerless, are marching in the streets, organizing in their communities, educating their people, and building movement for another world:

Thank you for your courageous actions, freedom fighter hearts, and tender humanity. Thank you for helping create a better world, through your truth telling, strategic engagement, and organizing to build collective power. A better word for our elders, for our children, for all of us.

To the white men, all of them white men, who have told me to burn in hell, to leave this country, and to die a horrible death. Let your hearts and minds be free of the poison of white supremacy, let go of the socialized hatred of imaginary dark-skinned enemies, and recognize that our humanity and future are bound together, and while racism drips from your tongue, it also holds your heart hostage,

Civil Rights organizer and legendary white anti-racist, Anne Braden, spoke of the "Other America" where people of all backgrounds come together to work for justice and democracy for all people. The "Other America" where we can live interdependently and cooperatively in our full humanity, with dignity. Reject the living hell of racism, and open your hearts to the "Other America." If not for yourselves, then for your children.

For all of us who know another world is possible, let the love of those who have come before us, who have taken on injustice, defied illegitimate power and, through their lives, created victories, legacies, poetry, culture, and traditions of resistance and liberation that we inherit, let their love and all they have passed on nourish and sustain us.

Let us, in these Black Lives Matter movement times, take risks, join with others, and create a culture of courage to help us challenge white supremacy and build up a world where all Black lives matter, and a world where we can all get free of anti-Black racism and supremacy systems.

Queers for BLM Direct Action in San Francisco, CA. Photo: Amanda Arkansassy Harris

❝...we can all get free..❞

An Anti-Racist Vision for White and Majority White Faith Communities

To become an anti-racist faith community, the key question, for a white/white majority community, is not, "How do we get people of color to join our faith community?" it is, "How can we make a prolonged, spiritually-rooted, engaged commitment to uprooting white supremacy within our community and take on-going collective action to challenge it in society?"

Unitarian Universalists March Against Police Brutality in New York City, NY.
Photo: Marranda Major

Our goal is not to have white people sit alongside a person of color so as to affirm that those white people aren't racist. Our goal is to build and be part of beloved community united to end structural oppression and unleash collective liberation in our congregations, houses of worship, faith communities, schools, neighborhoods, workplaces, and throughout society.

Our goal is to join hands across the divisions of racism in our faith and in our communities, find and affirm our humanity in each other, and join our hearts and minds to the task of destroying white supremacy in every worldview, policy, law, institution, and governing body of our society.

For our faith communities to be places of healing for people of color and white people from the nightmare of racism. For our faith communities to be places of nourishment for people of color and white people about the multiracial struggles of our people to advance economic, racial, and gender justice and the continual process of overcoming oppression within the movement on the journey to end oppression in society. For our faith communities to raise our children, of all backgrounds, to be freedom fighters and practitioners of liberation values.

"Our goal is to build and be part of beloved community united to end structural oppression..."

Jewish Leaders Take Direct Action for BLM in New York City, NY. Photo: Simone Zimmerman

For our faith communities to be spiritually alive, learning from and contributing to liberation cultures and legacies. For our faith communities to be welcoming homes for people of all colors, sexualities, classes, ages, abilities, genders, and citizenship statuses. For our faith communities to regularly be inviting us into and preparing us for courageous action for collective liberation, held in loving community for the long haul. Let our theologies and our faith communities be active agents in the world, to help us all get free, together.

Being A Good Ally Is Not the Goal

My goal isn't to be a great ally. My goal is the abolition of white supremacist capitalist patriarchy and the building up of multiracial democracy, economic, gender and racial justice for all and a world where the inherent worth and dignity of all people and the interconnection of life are at the heart of our cultures, institutions, and policies.

Jewish Voice for Peace March for BLM in Boston, MA. Photo: Jewish Voice for Peace

If being an ally is useful, at times, to further this shared movement vision, then be an ally and be effective. If bringing leadership is helpful, at times, bring it, and rock it. But overall, the underlying goal of this vision is to be a good comrade giving what I/ we can to the larger movement and to team liberation, of which we are part of. Strive to be a comrade with a political framework, committed to building up other people's leadership, building up collective power, being able to read situations and act for the best of our goals, rather then feeling like there is a formula to follow, and being able to love ourselves and our people. Let guidelines and politics guide us, rather then narrow and trap us.

Let us continue to grow and learn through lessons from theory applied to practice, in the messy, beautiful and nuanced reality of life. Let us be expansive while also being grounded. Eyes on the prize, hearts on fire, lead with values, compassion, and a fundamental belief, grounded in history, of everyday people's movements' ability to bend the arc of the universe towards justice and change what's politically possible, to make collective liberation a reality, step by step.

At the end of the day, what we call ourselves is less important then how we treat people, the values we practice, the goals and vision that guide us, and the beloved community we are building on the journey to all get free.

Towards the "Other America"

White supremacy, we're coming for you. Every day that your "just following or-
ders" violence and viciousness is exposed, and as the Black Lives Matter uprising
continues to spread, more and more white people are realizing the truth. We awaken
to the truth that white supremacy is poisoning our hearts, devouring our humanity,
and replacing the possibility of love and compassion with a life sentence of fear and
hatred. The truth that racism creates cultural, economic and political illiteracy, and
spiritual poverty in white communities. The truth that anti-racism and racial justice
means loving white people fiercely enough to love the white supremacy out of us and
unite our values and energy to movements for multiracial democracy, human dignity
and economic justice for all.

We will fight you white supremacy. We will fight for every European American child
that you work day in and day out to turn them into soldiers and supporters of this
murderous business as usual. We will fight you, for every body, of every color, that
you seek to steal, imprison, deprive, punish, exploit, narrow, and brutalize. We see the
monstrosity of capitalism that feeds on human life and the sacredness of the Earth,
the monstrosity of global economic apartheid that you serve and protect, and we are
coming to burn down the calm and calculated logic of justified atrocities at the core
of this system.

In our pain, heartbreak, and outrage, in the rain of our tears, we are remembering
who we are, and what it means to be fully human. Fully human in the interconnected
web of life, where all have inherent worth and dignity. We are freedom dreaming
beyond the nightmare of structural inequality and the death culture that rationalizes
and celebrates it. We are seeing our humanity reflected back to us in the defiance of
working class Black youth in Ferguson and Baltimore, of the white teenager who
recorded the police violence in McKinney, Texas and spoke out, in the refusal to stay
silent and demand "Say Her Name" and "Black Trans Lives Matter, in the white faith
communities taking actions and risks to break the code of white silence, and each
time we act, we are reclaiming our own humanity back in action.

We are white racialized people who know that Black Lives Matter means laying
siege to the operations of genocide. Operations first developed by ruling classes
in Europe to subjugate other European nations. The reservation system developed
by England to take land from the Irish, the economic strategy of wealthy elites in
Western Europe, exploiting Eastern European "subhuman races", all brought by a

colonizing and slave owner ruling class to the founding of the United States. Operations further developed by slave masters to divide African people amongst themselves and to divide hearts and alliances between enslaved Africans and indentured Europeans. We know that racism isn't biological, but socially constructed, and that legacies and cultures of liberation also shape who we are and who we yearn to be. We know that Black Lives Matter means ending the body breaking, soul crushing, life force stealing structures of institutional racism. And we know that a collective liberation vision with Black Lives Matter at the center, means we all get free, together.

For the Spring Valley high school student brutalized in class, for Sanda Bland, For Tamir Rice, For Reika Boy, for the three Black Trans women Elisha Walker, Ashton O'Hare and Kandis Capri all murdered within 24 hours of each other in unrelated events, for Trayvon Martin, for Oscar Grant, for Eleanor Bumpers a senior citizen shot dead by New York police in a raid on her apartment in 1984 for being four months late in rent, for Medgar Evers, for Emmett Till, for white anti-racists Viola Liuzzo and Rev. James Reeb, murdered by white racists and the Klan, for my sons River and August, for all of our children and our elders, and for Ella Baker and Anne Braden who teach us that another way is possible, who teach us how to organize and build movements, and who believe in us, as ancestors, as we continue the journey towards the "Other America". We are building and we will win.

Rally and Street Theater at SURJ Los Angeles White People For Racial Justice March.
Photo: Margot Dunlap

Appendix 1: To Get Involved with Showing Up for Racial Justice (SURJ)

SURJ is a national network of groups and individuals organizing white people for racial justice. Through community organizing, mobilizing, and education, SURJ moves white people to act as part of a multi-racial majority for justice with passion and accountability. We work to connect people across the country while supporting and collaborating with local and national racial justice organizing efforts. SURJ provides a space to build relationships, skills, and political analysis to act for change.

We live in a time of great hope and possibility, yet the potential for a just world for all of us is not possible when racism and oppression keep us divided. This can make us forget how closely connected we truly are.

Tom Moffett, Civil Rights Leader and Comrade of Anne Braden, at SURJ rally in Louisville, KY. Photo: Sonja Farah de Vries

Racism is still present throughout all of our contemporary institutions and structures. Racism is devastating to people of color and is closely intertwined with all systems of oppression. It robs all of us—white people and people of color—of our humanity. We honor and learn from the long history of people of color and white people who have been unrelenting in their struggles for racial justice, and ending all systems of oppression.

We are showing up to take our responsibility as white people to act collectively and publicly to challenge the manipulation of racist fear by the ruling class and corporate elite. We know that to transform this country we must be part of building a powerful multiracial majority to challenge racism in all its forms.

To get involved, visit www.showingupforracialjustice.org. To get text message updates on SURJ activity, text JUSTICE to 502-337-3643.

Acknowledgments

The writing in this book was fueled by the urgency of the Black Lives Matter movement erupting throughout the country, guided by the love and rage in my heart, grounded by my prayers to ancestors and the divine, and supported by a vast network of people, community groups, faith communities, and social justice institutions that have encouraged me to keep going.

I have a beautiful family with two magical little ones, River, who is four, and August, who was born just three months ago, while I worked on the book. That said, in the months since the people of Ferguson rose up, my writing has taken form standing in the aisles at the grocery store, in the parking lot of the YMCA (before and after working out), after taking my son to preschool, with my baby sleeping next to me, and most frequently, on my work days, channeling the emotions of these times into writing at the Green Hills library in Nashville. I pray, write, cry, look into the sky, and do rituals of gratitude for my comrades, known and unknown, all over the country, who are throwing down in enormous and courageous ways. This has been my spiritual practice. Throughout this journey, my partner, Jardana Peacock, has encouraged and supported me. The love and family we have created gives me life, and doing this work for collective liberation is deeply influenced by the beloved community our family is part of and the world I want our kids to grow up in.

As the essays, notes to activists and interviews began appearing, people started asking me to compile them for their activist groups to study, for their congregations to use, for giving out to white people showing up at their vigils and demonstrations, and for sharing with family and friends. Out of these requests, came the idea for this book.

There's no way I could have done this book without the team that came forward to help make it happen. Aisha Shillingford volunteered to work on the design and in the process has become the visual director of the project. Jake Dockter and Margaret Ernst co-edited the book and are now the co-directors of promotion. Getting a book together is daunting by itself. Add that to the life transforming experience of having a second child, and I often wondered how this was ever going to happen. The answer was having a team of brilliant, make-it-happen activists committed to the vision of the book being a resource to equip white people to show up and work for Black Lives Matter in these times. Aisha, Jake and Margaret, I'm so grateful for each of you.

While those unfamiliar with modern book publishing often think authors make a lot of money, the reality is, grassroots social justice authors often have to raise money to get their books published. Thank you so much to the people, organizations and faith communities that contributed money to help cover more then half of the production costs of the book. Thank you to Jewish Voice for Peace, Unitarian Universalist Congregation of Tuscaloosa, AL, Rev. Suzi Spangenberg, Axel and Elaine Gehrmann, Carla Wallace, Laurel Smith, Joseph Durham, Acadia Roher, Seth Newton Patel, Will Brummett, Tom Bozeman, John Varga, Kate Cardona, Rev. Fred Hammond, Stephanie Lane, Scott Prinster, Genevieve Ameduri, Rev. Ashley Horan, Benjamin Mauer, Marie Reed, Meck Groot, Leadership for Change Training and Consulting, Marian Urquilla, Mickey Ellinger, MarySue Foster, Rev. Jonathan Rogers, Jo Walter, Alexa Fraser, Shelly Tochluk, Keith Gallo, and Poa Zann Erick.

Thank you to all the incredible organizers and leaders who put considerable thought and time into the interviews in the book. In addition to those whose interviews appear in the book, I also want to give thanks to my comrades in Arkansas, Tennessee, North Carolina, Washington, and Missouri, who put energy into doing interviews, even if they were never finished. And thank you to all of the incredible photographers whose photos bring courage, defiance and hope alive throughout the book. While the vast majority of photos passed onto me were too low resolution to use, and we were unable to find higher quality images, I am grateful to the dozens of people who gave me photos. It's been inspiring seeing pictures of so many people taking action around the country.

Grateful for the feedback of Leslie Mac, Nora Rasman, and Drew MacFadyen on the essay "We Must Weather the Storm to See the Rainbow: An Open Love Letter to White Unitarian Universalists" and for the feedback of Liz Oppenheimer on the essay "An Anti-Racist Vision for White and Majority White Faith Communities. I am also thankful for the feedback of Atena Oyadi, Rahula Janowski, Nora Rasman, Attica Scott, Elandria Williams and my Facebook community, on the title of the book.

My dear friend, Allyn Steele, encouraged me to reach out to Steve Knight at Chalice Press and Steve responded enthusiastically from the beginning. I'm grateful to Chalice Press for jumping into this experiment of quickly publishing a free e-book and a print book that will just cover their expenses. They agreed, because they believe in the importance of getting the book out far and wide in faith communities and beyond.

There are many people who inspire me and whose work I see my own efforts moving alongside. I asked some of my closest people to be part of my Jedi Council for Collective Liberation. These are mentors, advisors, and comrades who I look to for guidance in my work and in my writing. Love and gratitude to my Jedi Council: Rev. Hope Johnson, Marc Mascarenhas-Swan, Tufara Waller Muhammad, Rahula

Janowski, Ingrid Chapman, Elandria Williams, Rev. Osagyefo Sekou, Molly McClure, Allyn Steele, Harsha Walia, Chris Dixon, Carla Wallace, Attica Scott, José-Antonio Orosco, Ash-Lee Woodard Henderson and the Anarres Project for Alternative Futures.

And finally, I want to give thanks to the millions of people who have taken to the streets and whose courage called me forward, time and time again, to write this book. In particular I want to thank Alicia Garza, Patrisse Cullors, and Opal Tometi of the Black Lives Matter organizing network who have brought tremendous, highly public, leadership. The courage these three freedom fighters bring to the work is contagious.

Towards the "Other America" is dedicated to Ella Baker and Anne Braden and the organizing tradition they have handed down to us. Ella Baker and Anne Braden have deeply influenced my entire approach to movement building and organizing for the past twenty years. They are ancestors who I feel with me when I lead a workshop or give a talk or a sermon. They are ancestors who I reach out to for courage when I'm scared and I try to do right by them in my work. I have written and taught about both of them for years, with the goal of passing on this tradition to new generations of leaders and organizers. This book comes out of their tradition.

Let us continue working together to build up the beloved community for my children to grow up in, for all of our children to grow up in, and for all of us to grow old in. Together we can. Forever we must.

Demouria Hogg Direct Action in Oakland, CA. Photo: Felicia Gustin

Rev. Julie Taylor prepares Unitarian Universalists for Civil Disobedience in St. Louis, MO.
Photo: Nora Rasman

About the Author

Chris Crass and Family at Ferguson Solidarity Rally in Nashville, TN.
Photo: Carmine Matlock

Chris Crass writes and speaks widely on anti-racist organizing, feminism for men, strategies to build visionary movements, and creating healthy culture and leadership for progressive activism. His first book, Towards Collective Liberation: Anti-Racist Organizing, Feminist Praxis, and Movement Building Strategy, draws lessons from his organizing over the past 27 years, along with case studies of historic and contemporary anti-racist organizing. His essays have been translated into half a dozen languages, taught in hundreds of classrooms, and published in over a dozen anthologies including Globalize Liberation: How to Uproot the System and Build a Better World, On the Road to Healing: An Anthology for Men Ending Sexism, and We Have Not Been Moved: Resisting Racism and Militarism in 21st Century America.

Chris was a founder of the Catalyst Project, which is a center for anti-racist/racial justice political education, leadership development, and multiracial movement building. Catalyst Project uses a collective liberation vision and strategy to help unite white communities to multiracial racial justice efforts. He was the co-coordinator of Catalyst Project from 2000-2011. Through Catalyst Project, Chris was part of the original cohort that helped launch the national network, SURJ (Showing Up For Racial Justice), which organizes white people to work for racial justice. He served on the SURJ leadership team and works with SURJ to connect white people around the country to the network, and supports local SURJ chapters through political education events. He is a speaker with Speak Out: The Institute for Democratic Education and Culture, which is dedicated to the advancement of education, racial and social justice, cultural in racy, leadership development and activism. Rooted in his Unitarian Universalist faith, Chris works with congregations, seminaries, and religious leaders to build up the spiritual/religious Left.

He lives in Nashville, Tennessee with his partner, Jardana Peacock and their sons River and August. You can learn more about Chris's work at www.chriscrass.org.

About the *Towards the "Other America"* Team

Visual Editor and Designer: Aisha Shillingford

Co-editors and Promotion Directors: Jake Dockter and Margaret Ernst

Originally from Trinidad and Tobago, **Aisha Shillingford** is a freelance artist, trainer, facilitator and social change strategist who has been living in Boston, MA for the past 16 years. With over 15 years of community organizing and program development experience in Boston, Aisha dreams of a day when we all believe that community really is the answer to every problem and when we are truly prefiguring the community we wish to see in our every day practices as change makers. She is pretty excited about the role of mestizaje and creolization in fostering cultural shift and is trying to get free. Aisha is a member of the creative collective, Intelligent Mischief.

Jake Dockter is a white anti-racist organizer and activist in Portland, OR. His main loves are his wife and daughter, who both inspire and challenge him daily. He also works as a new media and PR consultant and is a faith community organizer.

Margaret Ernst is a white, faith-rooted organizer currently living in Nashville, TN. A student of liberation movements, women's wisdom, and Christian social justice tradition, she formerly led communications for POWER, a Philadelphia-based organization affiliated with PICO National Network. She is in the process of seeking ordination in the United Church of Christ.

4/16

CPSIA information can be obtained
at www.ICGtesting.com
Printed in the USA
LVOW04s0135190116

471174LV00024B/1915/P